CROSS-COUNTRY
SKIING

CROSS-COUNTRY
SKIING
Touring and Competition

David Rees

Copp Clark Publishing
A Division of Copp Clark Limited
Vancouver Calgary Toronto Montreal

ISBN 0-7730-4024-2

Acknowledgements

Thanks are given to the following for the use of their photographs in this book.

Frank Cooke (pp. 5, 112)
Finnish Tourist Board (pp. 128-29)
Paul Leroux (pp. 164, 166)
Dave Lyseng (pp. 2, 6-7, 55, 76, 119, 126, 162, 168, 181, 182, 184-85, 191, 202)
Matti Maki (p. 147)
Norwegian National Tourist Office (front cover, pp. 124-25)
Jarl Omholt-Jensen (pp. 46-47, 100-101, 116-17, 121, 123, 145, 160, 165, 169, 171, 177, 180)
G. Rees (pp. 66, 67, 68, 69, 83 (*top*), 90 (*middle*), 93 (*top*), 140)
Eva Rossinger (p. 179)
M. Silver Associates (p. 10)
Swiss National Tourist Office (pp. ii, 1, 115)
Mike Whittington (pp. 107, 108)

Photographs on pp. 133, 138 are from P.O. Astrand and K. Rodahl, *Textbook of Work Physiology* (McGraw-Hill, 1970). Used with permission of McGraw-Hill Book Company.

All other photographs, including back cover photograph, and all drawings are by the author.

Copp Clark Publishing
517 Wellington Street West
Toronto, Ontario
M5V 1G1

Printed and bound in Canada

To my wife, Gail, who has never waivered
in her support of my skiing endeavours

Contents

Preface

A few decades ago, anyone who skied in North America was familiar with flexible boots, pine tar waxes, trail skiing, and climbing hills. Hardy souls gathered on crisp, clear winter mornings in crowded, noisy clubhouses amid the exciting smell of scorched pine tar from ski bottoms being run over the top of a big barrel stove, and made ready to race. Later in the day the more passive souls appeared with lunches and families for an afternoon of trail skiing and downhill running on some distant hardwood hill.

Then came the technological boom in the ski industry. Skis acquired steel edges, shiny, lacquered finishes, and plastic bottoms. Waxing became a thing of the past, and the old clubhouses gave way to plushly carpeted lounges, bars, and central heating. Skiers left the trails for the comfort and ease of the ski lifts, and cross-country skiing almost disappeared; almost, but not quite.

Through the efforts of an enthusiastic minority it survived, and over the past few years, in response to a growing awareness for the need for physical fitness and to a growing disenchantment with the expense and crowd of alpine skiing, it has once again become a popular sport. Now winter people are seeking an alternative to the crowded lift line or the soul-destroying roar of the snowmobile. They still want to do their own thing, operate as a family unit, and at the same time get fresh air, sun, and exercise. Cross-country skiing, as a perfect exercise and as a low-cost route to self-reliance and relaxation, has provided the alternative.

Herein lies the purpose of this book—to expose the simplicity and fullness of a reviving sport as well as to instruct converts and those returning to the sport in up-to-date equipment, technique, and waxing. For those both young and old who find challenge in competition, the second part of the book explains the elements of physiology, conditioning, and ski racing. Whether tourers or racers, all cross-country skiers experience the same basic regimen. They differ only in their approach and strategy. Thus the racer may well gain insight by reading part one and the tourer need not feel humble while reading part two. This book is for both.

Although I accept the responsibility for the words herein, credit must be given to Mr. Alex Isbister and Mr. Charles Kahn for their editorial work and to all those persons who supported and furthered my skiing career, especially Alex Stevenson, Frank Cooke, my parents, and my wife.

D.L.R.

CROSS-COUNTRY SKIING

PART ONE

Cross-Country Skiing for Fun

CHAPTER 1

What is it?

Although the term "cross-country skiing" is relatively new in North America, this type of skiing is thought to date back about five thousand years in Norway. Ancient skis found well preserved in a bog tell the story. Very wide and long, they were obviously used as a means of winter transport and travel rather than simply for leisure or sport. Made from pine, which abounds in Norway, they were apparently used both in peacetime and on warring excursions and, eventually, in this manner they found their way to other parts of the world.

The ski was an integral part of the equipment used by the heroes in many of the great Norwegian and Swedish sagas. Two of these sagas have been the inspiration behind the founding of world-renowned annual touring races in Scandinavia. In Norway the "Birkebeiner" commemorates the saving of young Haakon Haakonsson, heir to the throne of Norway, from potential usurpers by members of the King's Guard in 1215. They skied from Oslo to the safety of Trondheim, a distance of some three hundred miles. In Sweden the Vasaloppet each year retraces the route skied by King Gustaf (Vasa) Eriksson in 1521 when he fled from Salem to Mora, a distance of some 85 kilometres (53 miles) to escape from political assailants. Thus the ski is really part of Scandinavian culture, and it is a matter of great national pride and prestige to Scandinavians when their racers cross the finish line first in Olympic and other international events.

In North America we are still fledglings at the sport; cross-country skiing was not introduced here until the 1850s with the migration of Swedish and Norwegian workers to the mining and timber operations, which were booming at that time. Many of the newcomers had skied in the valleys and mountains of their homeland and brought with them a love of skis and snow. Many of them were legends in their time for their daring feats on skis. They were men such as "Snowshoe" Thompson who for twenty years carried the mail through the mountains of California to the gold fields, Adolf Olsen of Berlin Mills who was reported to have done a somersault on skis free of charge from the old jumphill in Rockcliffe Park in Ottawa, Sigurd and Hans Lockeberg who were prominent ski jumpers in the early 1900s, and of course the venerable ski legend of the Laurentians, Herman "Jackrabbit" Smith-Johansen of St. Sauveur, Quebec, who has skied across the country and is still skiing, at the age of ninety-eight.

Cross-country skiing consists essentially of sliding on skis over all sorts of terrain uphill and down, with the path restricted only by the places too steep to hold snow or by the trees themselves. More specifically it is a means of walking on skis, which for the novice may begin as a shuffling of the legs and feet, one ahead of the other by means of sliding or lifting the skis along the surface of the snow. Through practice, patience, and experience, the novice can develop this awkward stumble into a smooth, rhythmical, push-slide sequence, moving over the snow in much the same manner as a figure skater glides over the ice. In the case of the skater, one leg and foot kicks down and to the rear propelling him forward, while the other leg and foot supports his weight as it glides on the blade of the skate. Similarly, in cross-country skiing, a downward and backward "kick" of one leg propels the skier forward while his weight is supported by the other.

However cross-country skiing and ski touring are much more than just a mechanical to-and-fro motion of the lower limbs or just a physical effort of the individual to propel himself across the snow. They are really a way of life for many people, a recreation, a sport, a competition, a challenge, and eventually they even capture the soul. Even after many outings, the experience, the freedom of gliding over the snow on a

Cross-country skiing

well-packed trail with body, mind, and skis working well, gives one a tremendous feeling of health and well-being.

Cross-country skiing, as practised in North America, has two main aspects— touring and racing. Touring, in essence, is hiking over rolling country on skis for a few hours, a day, or even overnight. The idea is to ski from place to place, maybe stopping for lunch, enjoying the sun and the fresh air and taking a little exercise for your health. No special skills, only a basic knowledge of technique and waxing, are required to enjoy ski touring. As soon as you are equipped you can join your friends on the trail or sneak off into the solitude of the winter woodland by yourself for a quiet day's outing.

Cold feet in cross-country skiing are a myth. Even the coldest feet will find warmth in the activity and effort required to navigate the smoothest of terrain. Nevertheless, this doesn't mean that you can stand around in cross-country ski boots for prolonged periods in the snow. Even the best in winter footwear will produce cold feet if you stand too long in the cold, but as long as you are engaged in skiing there is nothing to fear from the cold.

Cross-country skiing is definitely not a passive pursuit, but on the other hand it is not one which demands excruciating physical work either, as many people tend to believe. Alpine skiers who have undergone the agony of trying to climb hills in fresh, deep, powder snow with their heavy assortment of alpine skiing hardware may be responsible for the misconception. Their fixed, heavy boots and rigid bindings make the flexing of the ankles (necessary for easy climbing) difficult. Cross-country equipment is light and pliable and special cross-country ski waxes prevent the skis from sliding backward down the hill, so that the skier doesn't usually end up in a pile of arms, legs, skis, and poles because his skis have lost their purchase on the slope. As a result of these special waxes and light-weight equipment, cross-country skiing is really only as much work as you choose to make it.

The effort that you put in will be a measure of your reward. However, even small efforts in cross-country skiing reap large rewards in your health and well-being because the exercise that you do is an ideal form of aerobic conditioning that builds vital body systems such as the circulation, the heart, and the lungs. As modern man becomes more and more sedentary in his habits such conditioning is becoming more necessary to maintain good health and to prevent possible early death due to a weak heart. In fact some Swedish researchers contend that cross-country racers in their population tend to live on the average ten years longer than other citizens. Such rewards, coupled with sunshine, fresh air, and friendship, provide a very healthy form of recreation both physically and mentally.

Racing is something else. Cross-country ski racing is one of those sports where the performance is highly dependent on physical conditioning and training. The skier must be prepared to undertake hard, exhaustive work. Training is a major part of the ski racer's diet, maybe as high a proportion as 60 to 80 per cent with the remaining 20 to 40 per cent's being the mastery of technique. Of course, there are naturally gifted people who have seemingly unlimited endurance and need to train less than their peers, but the general rule is that

Ski touring

if you are willing to work harder than the next person then eventually your performance will be better.

Cross-country skiing is also an attractive family sport. A relatively low financial outlay will equip the entire family. The only absolute essentials are skis, bindings, boots, poles, and wax. Special clothing is not required and fancy gadgetry is an active detriment. The cross-section of ages usually found in the family is no barrier to family participation. The sport accom-

modates people of all ages and abilities, allowing the family to ski as a group. Even the family dog can be included in a cross-the-fields tour.

Little or no coaching or instruction is necessary to begin to fully enjoy the sport of cross-country skiing because it is as natural as walking. Snow abounds in most regions and temperatures in mid-winter are seldom absolutely unbearable so why should we sit indoors and lament over the length of the winter? Why not enjoy the winter and be part of it by cross-country skiing?

Cross-country skiing can be practised virtually anywhere. No lifts are required and even the absence of hills is not a deterrent.

Just a few inches of snow on a football field or a golf course is an adequate cover for cross-country skiing. Indeed, too much snow can sometimes make for heavy going though there is an incomparable thrill in running downhill in virgin, snowy fields with the snow flowing over your ankles. In reality any amount of snow will do as long as there is enough to allow the skis to slide.

Skiers right in the heart of some of the largest urban centres in North America—New York, Toronto, and Montreal—seek out the space in parks to pursue their sport. Likewise, some university teams use the football field, covered with just a bit more than a heavy, frozen dew, to practise technique in order to get the jump on their

Age, size, and ability are no barrier to the enjoyment of skiing

rivals in the fall. Many of the city parks are ideal because they are lighted by the diffuse city glow produced by the cars and street lights. In fact some are so well lighted that night races have been held in them with the addition of extra lighting only at crucial points.

On the whole, however, cross-country skiing is practised away from the hustle of urban life, in the wilderness or at least in wooded areas and woodlots semi-isolated from traffic and noise. As a rule cross-country enthusiasts tend to be rather sensitive to noise and crowds—maybe because they have experienced the freedom of the wide open spaces and unobstructed paths. As a result they seek out semi-isolated spots for their clubhouses and trails.

In rural areas of course such privacy is no problem to find, although an alarming increase in the popularity and dispersion of snow machines is becoming a consternation to some skiing enthusiasts. Many choice trails in these rural areas follow old logging roads that have been long abandoned for winter use by trucks. Such roads offer a variety of terrain and well-cleared downhills where dense bush has been removed, offering a safe descent.

In farming country open fields provide wide vistas and interesting terrain. Skiing over fields and fences has come to be known as "cross-lots" or "cross-patch" skiing. Conversely, picking a path through the forest has come to be known as "bushwhacking". Bushwhacking can be hard on equipment, but in providing a sure test of ability at dodging trees, bumps, and gullies, it can be a great deal of fun. Never-

theless such cavorting is not recommended until you have mastered the use of the skis and until you have developed a delicate feel for the limitations and fragility of your equipment.

Snow conditions seldom present frustration either. Sloppy wet snow, the curse of alpine skiers because of its unrelenting suction on the ski bottom, can be made problem free by the amazing properties of cross-country ski wax. Cross-country wax allows a person to ski straight up a hill and just as easily slide down the other side. If the proper wax for the prevailing conditions is selected, then skiing will be relatively easy. The skis will not slip back, so no elaborate climbing technique will be required. Waxing can be fun. It provides an additional challenge for the skier and at the same time it makes him aware of the vagaries of the weather and the associated varieties of snow. As well it provides the basis for much conversation (and controversy) on the mixing and applying of the various combinations in a search for the best one.

In summation, cross-country skiing provides a relatively inexpensive and wholesome pursuit, which is particularly amenable to our North American climate. From near obscurity it has begun to return as a form of winter recreation that allows maximum interaction between man and his natural environment. It provides a means of healthy exercise in natural surroundings at a pace anyone can enjoy. In the future it will likely continue to grow as more and more people seek refuge from automobile exhaust and urban madness.

CHAPTER 2

Equipment

Various brands and types of cross-country skis

A few years ago cross-country skis and skiing equipment were not so readily available as they are now, and many people improvised. Solid maple, birch, or hickory alpine skis were planed down to widths similar to that of the cross-country ski and rigged up with either a loose-fitting cable binding or with some sort of antique toe-clamp device. Boots consisted of old worn-out army boots or an ancient, weather-beaten, leather alpine boot that had lost all of its rigidity. Poles were fabricated from lengths of bamboo fishing-pole, filled with wooden plugs on the ends and fitted with a strap riveted or wired on. For the pointed end a screw nail was driven into the wooden plug, cut off and filed sharp. Ski-pole baskets were scavenged from alpine equipment. All in all such an assemblage

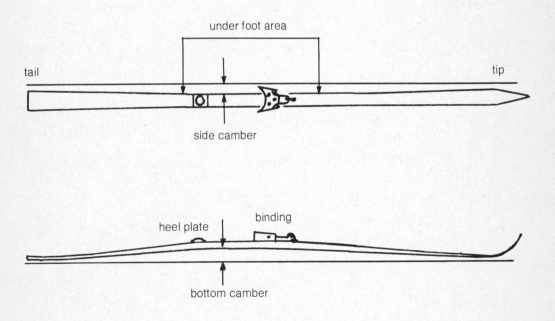

Figure 2.1   Ski Terminology

would present a very formidable selection in view of today's technologically tempered equipment but in times when money was scarce such improvisation was a necessity. Nevertheless, savings on money were often overshadowed by malfunctioning equipment, and many an enthusiast became disgusted and disillusioned after losing the same ski five or six times during a cross-country race.

The basic assemblage needed today by a beginner consists of skis, harness, boots, poles, and wax. Clothing at first is no problem. Ordinary, loose-fitting clothing that provides some protection against the cold is quite suitable at the start, though later on some of the items mentioned in this chapter will be of interest.

Most cross-country ski equipment is Fenno-Scandian, and you will identify some interesting brand names on skis and boots that give the sport an international flavour. Competition among the "home" countries is fierce, and Scandinavian racers seldom use skis made in a rival country. In Europe and North America the brands are more equally dispersed, and choice becomes a matter of preference instead of national pride. It is interesting however that experienced skiers are often influenced by the brand of their favourite skis to be rooters for that nation's competitors on the international circuit.

Prices vary for equipment, but the basics can be purchased for sixty to ninety dollars. The lowest prices are usually found at shops that handle Nordic ski equipment exclusively, though many alpine shops, and even hardware stores, now are stocking an adequate range of equipment.

Be sure to start with good equipment. The few dollars you can save by settling for lower quality can mean warped skis or boots that won't break in. With this guideline, let's have a detailed look at each piece of equipment.

Skis

Cross-country skis are quite different from downhill skis, mainly because they have a different function. The downhill ski must be heavy (usually metallic), edged with steel, and relatively stiff in order to accommodate the high speed and icy conditions of the ski hill. Such conditions are not usually found on the ski trail, so cross-country skis can be made much lighter, narrower (no need for a steel edge) and most flexible.

Cross-country skis function as snow-shoes to help the skier from sinking too deeply into the snow and also as sliding platforms on which the skier can move over the snow. Thus they must be long enough and strong enough to support the weight of the skier and yet still perform in a torsional, flexible manner to slide over even the most bumpy and uneven terrain without breaking.

Types Cross-country skis come in various widths and flexes geared to different functions. Basically there are competition skis *(langren)* for use only on well-prepared tracks, light touring skis *(tur langren)* for the beginning and average skier, general touring skis *(tur)* used for heavy bushwhacking, and finally mountain skis, used in rough, icy conditions, especially in alpine areas. Each of these skis can be readily identified, mainly by differences in width and weight. Other more subtle differences can be found in their fabrication and in the materials used (see table 2.1).

Materials and Construction Most cross-country skis are made from wood, although now they are beginning to be made from fibreglass and plastics. Even so, it is unlikely that wood will be totally replaced due to its relatively low cost and ease of working. The main woods used are birch,

Table 2.1

Type	Width		Construction	Weight/Pair	Character
1. Racing: (Langren)	Special	*47 mm	Wood with 26 laminations or fibreglass	1.2-1.4 kg (3 lbs.)	light and flexible
	Regular	48 mm	Wood with 20 - 23 laminations or fibreglass	1.5-1.7 kg (3.7 lbs.)	somewhat heavier than special
2. Light Touring (Tur Langren)		50-51 mm	Wood with 19 - 22 layers or fibreglass	2.0 kg (4.5 lbs.)	stronger than racing skis
3. General Touring		52+ mm	Wood with 14 - 22 layers	2.2 kg + (5.5 lbs.)	for off track conditions
4. Mountain Skis		60 mm	Wood with 22 layers	3.0 kg + (6.7 lbs.)	usually have steel edges for icy conditions

*Ski-width measured under foot

spruce, hickory, ash, and balsa, and each type of ski will have different combinations and amounts of these woods. Usually spruce is found in the core, with birch, hickory, and ash as laminations around it. Birch often makes up the sole and top of the ski, although for some skis a sole of hickory provides extra strength and durability. Inlaid along the edges of the birch sole often there is a hickory or lignostone (oil-soaked, compressed beech) edge. Competition skis have the added feature of a hollow, channelled core or a balsa core. Synthetics such as plastic and fibreglass have been employed to strengthen key spots such as the tip, tail, and underfoot sections of the ski and lately have also been used to improve the sliding surface. Recently, fibreglass ski construction has been perfected, and there is a selection of racing and light touring skis available in this material as well.

Brands From Finland you will recognize such ski brands as Finn-skis, Karhus, Rex, and the big seller in North America, Jarvinen. From Norway come durable skis under the trade names of Bla skia, Bonna, Trysil Knut, Kongsberg, Splitkein, Telemark, Toppen, Madshus, and Landsem, with Madshus, Landsem, Toppen, and Splitkein being most popular in North America. Swedish ski production is centred at Edsbyn in one huge factory, which produces Edsbyn, Sundin, and Sandstrom skis. Worthy of note are two other skis made in Sweden and Germany, the Montana and Trak touring skis. The Montana has a P-Tex plastic base with a mohair insert under the foot region, while the Trak ski has a fish-scale-like plastic surface. Both skis are reputed to operate without waxing. Fischer and Kneissel of Austria also make a completely fibreglass ski with a plastic base.

There are several domestic skis. Of note are the ABC ski of Montreal and the Rastas ski, an extremely durable and well-made hand-crafted ski made in Sault Ste. Marie, Ontario. Neither one of these skis is mass produced.

The best makes of racing skis from the three Scandinavian countries are pretty well matched, that is, if you can obtain an extremely good pair. In the past, however, the policy of some ski manufacturers has been to ship only the mediocre skis to North America. Now that North American skiers are becoming much more proficient, they are demanding better quality, but the best skis are still removed from the stock at the factory to supply the home national teams and a few other top racers. Of the wooden skis, Norwegian touring skis have a tendency to be stronger, but also a little heavier and stiffer, than Swedish or Finnish touring skis. Finnish skis tend to have sharply upturned tips with rounded upper surfaces, whereas Norwegian and Swedish skis have flat upper surfaces.

The Ski Bottom The choice of ski bottom must suit the use that you intend to give the skis. The requirements will vary for the beginner, occasional skier, enthusiast, and racer. Some of the options are discussed below.

Experience has shown that most beginners, unfamiliar with skiing and skis, tend to ski, at times uncontrollably, over all types of debris, ice, sand, etc., and generally tend to neglect wax and ski care. Usually the skis take quite a beating under such use. Thus beginners need a good durable bottom on the ski, and in wood the best is hickory, recognized by its open, coarse grain. Couple the hickory with a lignostone edge and you have a ski for all conditions. Although a birch bottom with hickory edges is a popular combination for ski soles, it is not recommended for other than ideal

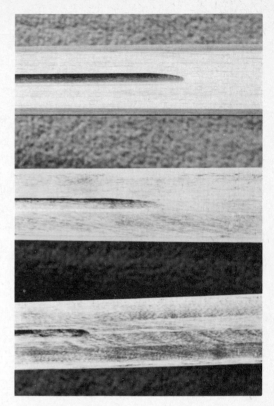

Three types of wood bottoms: (top to bottom) hickory with lignostone edge, birch with plastic edge, and birch with hickory edge

Hickory bottom, lignostone edge—a good combination for the touring skier

conditions of powder or soft snow, because as a fairly soft wood, birch soon wears and pits under harsh crusty or icy conditions.

Synthetic materials such as fibreglass make very durable ski bottoms and take much abuse, but often the material has a tendency to be too rigid, and eventually hairline fractures develop across the ski width under the continual flexing imposed by trail conditions. Few synthetics hold wax very well, and soft plastics found on some ski bottoms may require waxing several times during a tour. Nevertheless, there are some advantages to synthetics in that the ski bottom is entirely waterproofed and requires very little maintenance.

Some recent developments in synthetic bottoms feature a plastic fish-scale texture over the whole ski, or mohair under the foot for climbing. No wax is required for climb-ing, and they do work, but slide is reduced considerably and the fish-scale bottom tends to wear quickly. Once the lips have worn off the scales, the skis are useless. They cannot be waxed easily and the grip is gone unless the bottom is replaced. The mohair strips, on the other hand, can be replaced easily. However, for the most part, dedicated enthusiasts who use their skis daily or several times per week prefer wood and wax over these features.

An epoxy-tar bottom is also available on racing skis. This material provides an excellent waterproof sole on the ski and holds wax better than the smooth plastics. The epoxy-tar bottom has proved to be faster than wood, especially in damp or wet conditions. Unfortunately it is rather soft and does not have the durability for a general use ski.

Table 2.2   Recommended Ski Choice

Use	Beginner and Occasional Skier	Enthusiast	Racer
Trail	Light touring with hickory sole and lignostone edge *or* Light touring with plastic fish scale or mohair sole.	Light touring or Regular racing—with hickory or birch sole and hickory or ligno-stone edge.	Special racing—birch or epoxy-tar sole—with hickory edges.
Off Trail	General touring with hickory bottom and lignostone edge *or* General touring with plastic sole and mohair strip.	Light touring—hickory sole with or without ligno-stone edge.	Regular racing—for deep snow training—epoxy-tar or hickory sole with lignostone edge.
Alpine Touring		Mountain skis with hickory or plastic sole and steel or aluminum edge.	

Choosing the Proper Ski Types, lengths, and construction of skis have been outlined above. The problem is, what combination of these features should you look for? Generally, it is best to try to select a ski to suit your purpose, ability, and experience. Some hints and recommendations are given below.

If you are a beginner, try to stay away from birch bottoms and balsa or air cores, because of the lack of strength and durability introduced by these features. Plastics are durable, but still have their drawbacks, both structurally and economically. Wood is still the best and cheapest all-round material for general cross-country skiing and touring. If you are only an occasional skier, the no-wax, synthetic-bottom skis may perform well enough for you, but if you plan to use your skis a great deal then you had best select a hickory-bottom ski with lignostone edges for durability. If your purpose is to compete, then you will want to choose a light-weight, flexible racing ski with an epoxy-tar bottom, a birch bottom with a hickory edge, or a fibreglass bottom.

Mountain skis, which are quite wide, heavy, and very stiff, should not be considered for general touring. They are recommended only for mountain conditions where part of the tour may involve alpine ski conditions and the width and strength of the ski are required for high-speed downhill running. Often dealers try to sell these wider models to unsuspecting beginners because they feel that the wider ski will provide more stability for the beginner, but the extra weight and stiffness, if anything, add to the beginner's problems, because they decrease the ease of manipulation. In addition, heavier harnesses and boots are required for such skis, and for an ordinary through-the-woods outing such extra weight really offers no advantage.

Choosing the Proper Ski Length The traditional method of determining proper ski length is still used in selecting cross-country skis. For skis to be deemed the proper length, the tip of the upright ski should reach to the wrist of the arm extended upward. Of course, such an assessment doesn't allow for the skier's weight or ability and in a lot of situations, especially with respect to tall persons, the measure becomes ridiculous. Many persons over six feet tall can reach upward of 245 cm, which represents a length more suitable in a jumping ski. In selecting a proper length you must keep in mind that the ski must support your weight on the snow without sinking too deeply or breaking, so if you are on the heavy side, then a little longer ski might be better and vice versa. Generally speaking, the longer the ski, the stronger it is and the more weight it will hold. There is a considerable increase in strength in skis that are longer than 210 cm, but of course there is also an increase in the ski weight. Hence persons who are tall and heavy should select a ski perhaps 215 or 220 cm long. If you plan to use your skis always on packed trails then the ski can be a little shorter; on the other hand, if you plan to do only bushwhacking and deep-snow wandering you could add 5 cm onto your normal ski length.

To choose the proper length for you, begin by selecting good-quality skis from the pile of a length about one foot greater than your height. Then test each pair for stiffness as outlined below and select the pair best suited to your weight. Persons well over six feet in height should begin testing skis of lengths 215 to 220 cm. Most likely they will need these lengths to guarantee the strength in the ski that they will require.

Generally, the most popular lengths are 205 and 210 cm for men between 5'8" and 6'1" or 6'2" in height and with weights ranging from 150 to 180 lbs. For women,

Table 2.3

| Height | | | Ski Length | Pole Length |
Ft.	In.	Cm	Cm	Cm
4'	2"	125	150	100 - 110
	6"	135	160	110 - 115
	9"	145	170	115 - 120
	11"	150	180	120 - 125
5'	1"	155	185	125 - 130
	3"	160	190	130 - 135
	5"	165	195	135 - 140
	7"	170	200	140 - 142.5
	9"	175	205	142.5 - 145
	11"	180	210	145 - 150
6'	1"	185	215	150 - 155
	3"	190	215-220	152.5 - 160

For Ski Length: Add 30 cm to your height and select stiffness for weight.

For Pole Length: Subtract 25-30 cm from your height and adjust up or down to preference.

190 and 195 cm are popular lengths, but, again, if you are taller and heavier than average you may need a longer or stiffer ski. Table 2.3 gives a guide to the length of ski one should have—note that the ski lengths are graduated in units of 5 cm and the maximum production-line length is 220 cm. Adjustments can be made up or down for ski length if you are heavier or lighter than the normal weight for your height.

By now you have probably realized that no hard and fast rules exist for the matching of ski length to skier. One must consider weight, height, and ability in ski selection. Often it is helpful to consult other skiers of your own height and build and ask to look at their skis. Ask them how they are performing and look for the subtle hints on the ski bottom (outlined below) that give away just how well the ski is suited to the skier. Often such conversations are ex-

tremely useful even to experienced competitors when they are trying to select a proper stiffness from a new brand of ski that they have not tried before. It also goes without saying that experience, and trial and error will soon educate the skier to which equipment is best suited to his experience, ability, and technical prowess.

Choosing Proper Stiffness Each ski length has a range of stiffnesses from a soft flex to a fairly stiff flex; the degree of stiffness in the ski may condition your choice of ski length. As mentioned earlier, a heavier skier may want a longer ski to support his extra weight, but if he finds the extra length unmanageable then he has an alternative. He can select a stiffer pair of skis. Stiffness generally means a stronger ski, but one must be careful, because prolonged exposure to hot and dry conditions can dry out the ski and also make it stiff. Such a ski, when exposed again to the snow, will reabsorb moisture and soften considerably. Try to determine the immediate history of the skis that you are evaluating before deciding about stiffness, and always leave some leeway for a slight softening when the ski is used on the snow several times.

It is important that the ski support your weight along its whole length. If you are not heavy enough to press the skis to the floor at their middle then most of your weight is being taken by the tips and tails, which will invariably result in the premature wearing out of these two areas. Conversely, if the ski is too soft in the middle, then it will wear badly in the section beneath your foot. When the ski bottom wears to a white patch in either of these areas your skis' stiffness and your weight are not in harmony.

The Hand Test Place the skis sole to sole, with tip to tip and attempt to squeeze the two skis together at their middle with one hand. If you can squeeze them together and remove all of the camber from the skis with mild exertion using one hand, then the skis are most likely of the proper stiffness to hold your weight on the snow. If the skis close too easily then they are too soft, and, conversely, if they do not close at all, then they are too stiff. Although not an accurate test, this one, after practice and experience, can be useful when you are trying to select a reasonable pair of skis from a large stock.

The Paper Test   Once you have selected a pair as above, you can then place them on the floor or a flat surface with a sheet of paper under the mid section. Stand on them or weight them and try to pull the paper out. If the paper will not budge, then the ski is too soft; if the paper is too loose, then the ski is too stiff. The ski is just right for you if the paper comes free with a firm pull.

Choosing Quality   All pairs of skis issuing from a factory production line are not necessarily of similar quality even though they may be the same model. Variations in wood quality, gluing, and matching practices tend to produce differences in ski quality. Poorly seasoned wood or knotty wood may produce twisted or weakened skis; non-uniform spreading of glue on lamination surfaces may result in later separation of laminations and splitting; or skis may be improperly paired for similarity of weight and flex. All of these factors, along with others such as shipping and storage practices, will have a bearing on the quality of the ski that reaches the retailer and finally the consumer. Thus the consumer should know just what qualities to look for in a ski that is suitable for his weight, height, and ability. We have already discussed the type of ski, its fabric, and its length, so now we shall discuss one of the structural qualities to look for—things such

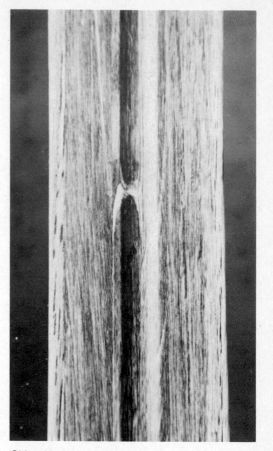

Skis with uneven grain may develop splits such as this

as signs of weakness, ski flex, and straightness.

Materials Check   First of all, a quick but complete visual inspection should be made of the ski and its running surface or sole for imperfections in material and workmanship. Knots should not appear in the wood on the sole or tips and tails of the ski because they represent points of weakness and a possible future break. You should, if possible, check the wood grain on the sole to be sure that it runs from the ski tip to the ski

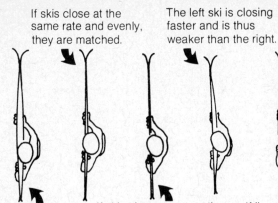

If skis close at the same rate and evenly, they are matched.

The left ski is closing faster and is thus weaker than the right.

If skis don't come fully together in their middle, they are too stiff.

Skier sights along ski with left eye.

If ski soles come together in a straight line, then skis are all right.

If line of contact of ski soles is not straight, then skis are warped.

The skis are straight, but the tips have opened up—an undesirable characteristic.

Figure 2.2   Ski Test: Straightness

tail (the direction of slide) in a reasonably continuous and straight pattern. Wood grains running in the opposite direction tend to disrupt the sliding surface, causing excess friction and poor slide, in addition to making the ski sole less durable. Skis with more obvious imperfections, such as splits and chips, should be rejected from the start. After the craftmanship of the skis has been checked, you can employ several simple but effective techniques to test the skis for structural quality and strength as well as suitability to your requirements. Most of these tests are outlined in the following pages.

Straightness Test   By squeezing the skis together and sighting with the eye from the tails forward along the ski length, one can further test the skis for straightness and other features. Both skis should close at the same rate and with the same diminishing amount of arc (figure 2.2). If one ski flattens more quickly than the other, then the skis are not of equal strength or stiffness. They are not a matched pair. Once closed together, if the line of contact between the ski soles is not a straight line,

then the skis are warped or twisted along their length and are not acceptable. Mind you, some skiers argue that a certain amount of twist is not unbearable and that it can be easily adjusted on wooden skis, but why not start out with a perfectly straight ski? Then there are no problems of trying to correct the twists. More sensitive skiers feel that a twisted ski does not grip the snow so well as a straight one and may cause unnecessary side action in the kick. Nevertheless, the argument still holds, that if you are going to invest some capital in cross-country ski equipment don't settle for second- or third-rate equipment. Be selective.

Spread Tips Test   Another malfunction to watch for is the action of the ski tips while closing the skis at eye level. Quite often the ski soles tend to separate at the tips for a foot or so when the middles of the soles are pressed together. This characteristic is also undesirable, because it prevents the skis from following the track well (tracking) on the snow. When you press down in the middle of the ski the tips tend to come up off the snow and on a choppy track it will seem as though you are striding on a field of ball bearings.

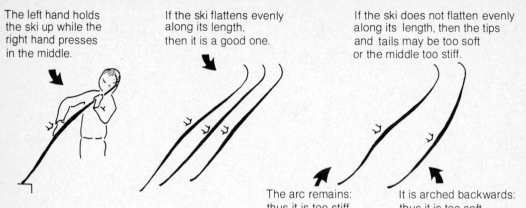

The left hand holds the ski up while the right hand presses in the middle.

If the ski flattens evenly along its length, then it is a good one.

If the ski does not flatten evenly along its length, then the tips and tails may be too soft or the middle too stiff.

The arc remains: thus it is too stiff here.

It is arched backwards: thus it is too soft or weak here.

Figure 2.3   Ski Flex

Ski Flex   "Ski flex" is a term used to describe how stiffness varies along the ski length. It is an important ski quality, because it will determine to some extent the wear pattern of the ski sole, the efficiency of the grip or slide of the wax, and ski performance.

By squeezing the skis together as you did to check for straightness, you can also check to see if the soles in mid ski come fully into contact with each other. If they do not, and a small amount of arc remains under the middle of each ski, then the skis are much too stiff in their midsections. If your weight is unable to press this stiff midsection onto the snow, then this particular pair of skis will tend to have backslip even with proper wax (figure 2.2).

An additional test can be applied by placing the ski tip in the left hand and pushing on top of the ski in its middle with the right hand to try to flatten it (figure 2.3). The eye should be at the ski tip sighting down along the edge of the ski to observe the flattening of the ski. The curvature should disappear quickly from the tips and tails, but should require a greater pressure to be removed from the midsection. In a good ski the arc will disappear from the midsection last and just at the point when the rest of the ski becomes straight. If the midsection does not lose its curvature until the tip and tail begin to bend upward, then either the midsection is too stiff or the extremities of the ski are too soft.

A ski with a flexible tip and a rather stiff tail is important in cross-country racing and is also comfortable for touring. A flexible tip tends to ride over bumps in the ski track smoothly, whereas a stiffer tip tends to push against the bump, momentarily resisting any forward motion of the ski, producing a rather abrupt action in the ski. The tail should be somewhat stiffer than the tip so that it effectively propels the ski forward as it slides down the forward side of the bump. Many of these ski tests may seem a little superfluous, but if you select a good ski of the proper flex, length, and weight, you will find that the skis will tend to track better, follow the trail almost without direction from you, and will allow the wax to perform much better as well. Once again be selective.

Ski Camber   Skis have two cambers, bottom and side camber, and a good ski must have adequate amounts of both. Bottom

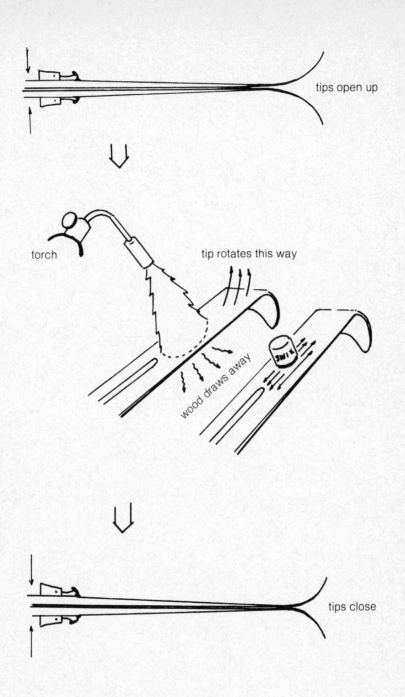

tips open up

torch

tip rotates this way

wood draws away

SWIX

tips close

Figure 2.4: Correcting Spread Tips

Correcting for

(a) excessive stiffness　　　　　　　(b) lack of stiffness

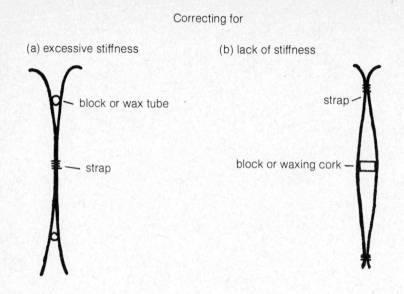

block or wax tube

strap

strap

block or waxing cork —

Figure 2.5

camber, the space between the two skis at mid length when they are placed sole to sole, should be about two inches. Side camber, or the amount the ski curves from the tips into the centre along the edges, is much less than bottom camber. It should be just enough to be noticeable.

Both cambers are necessary to provide good tracking ability. The arch under the ski, the bottom camber, prevents the ski from pivoting sideways when it is flattened onto the snow, and the arc along the edges provides stability for cornering when the wider tips and tails of the ski bite into the snow before the narrower mid ski.

Ski Adjustments　Many of the above ski imperfections can develop after the ski has been used for some time. Certain clues, such as wear patterns on the ski sole, will indicate how well a ski is performing during use. If the ski or ski wax wears excessively under the midsection of the ski, then the ski is too soft and not stiff enough to distribute the skier's weight evenly along its length on the snow. If the ski wears on the tips and/or tails, then the skis are too stiff and the skier's weight is not sufficient to press the ski onto the snow evenly along its length, so that the middle of the ski is seldom on the snow, bearing weight. If uneven wear patterns tend to persist, then something must be done before the ski is ruined. If you do happen to get stuck with a faulty pair of skis and you don't have the heart to unload them on some other poor unsuspecting soul, all is not lost. Adjustments can be made using only a blow torch and ski wax, if the imperfections are not too extreme.

Spread Tips　Spread ski tips, oftentimes the cause of wobbly or poorly tracking skis, can be brought back together by heating the ski sole about six to twelve inches from the ski tip and rubbing green Swix or some other hard wax over the heated area (figure

2.4). The heating serves two purposes: first, to cause the wood to draw away from the heat, and secondly, to open the wood pores to allow the wax to impregnate the wood. As the heated area becomes hot the wood draws away forcing the tips together again. The wax cools and hardens to hold the impregnated wood fibres rigid and thus keeps the tips together. It should be pointed out that this practice provides only a temporary adjustment of the ski tips, which might last one or two outings. Worthy of mention here is that ski bottoms burn readily, so you will want to be extremely careful with the torch. One good rule is to keep enough wax on the ski so that you can see bubbles forming—the wax will be absorbing the heat and preventing the wood from scorching. Dry wood burns much quicker than waxed wood.

Stiff or Soft Skis　Skis that are too stiff can be temporarily softened by heating the top of the skis, particularly in the midsection, and then strapping them together tightly with blocks jammed between the skis at each end (figure 2.5). After twenty-four hours or so, the skis will have temporarily lost some of their camber and stiffness. If this procedure proves to be ineffective, then it is possible to scrape the ski bottoms to remove some wood, thus weakening the ski and softening its flex. But such a practice can be dangerous, in that excessive removal of wood will change the structural strength of the ski and subsequent breakage may result. Exercise caution to ensure that your scraper is truly a straight edge and that you remove wood shavings evenly along the ski.

When a pair of skis is too soft, heat the ski soles and place a block between the skis in the region where your heel rests on the ski while skiing and strap the tips and tails together.

Restoring the Ski Sole　Attempts have been made to plane the edges and bottoms of well-worn skis, which may have become favourites with the skier, in an attempt to restore them. Except for a small amount of scraping with a flat steel or glass plate, this practice is not recommended for most cross-country skis. The veneer of birch or hickory on the ski sole is usually just thick enough and strong enough to prevent breakage. When this veneer is weakened through removal of wood, then of course the whole ski is weakened. Planing of the ski edge may restore the sharpness of the edges, but unless you are trained in ski manufacturing you may destroy the side camber of the ski, which is so important to the tracking and turning quality of the ski. A better practice is to keep clear of rocks and stubs in the first place, to keep your edges from getting too scraped and banged.

Extreme gouges and splits can be repaired with slow-drying epoxy glue mixed with sawdust or small wood chips. Be sure to remove all wax and scrape the gouge out to bare, fresh wood to ensure maximum contact between wood and glue. Once dry the glue can be sanded smooth with fine sand paper.

If you are industrious and have the tools and the time it is possible to fully refurbish the ski bottom. First chisel a very thin layer of wood from the full length of the ski bottom between the edges and then spread in a thin layer of epoxy-tar repair kit. When the epoxy compound is dry, carefully sand the bottom, using a flat block wrapped in sand paper, gradually levelling every part of the sole to the edges. Although not so tough as the original bottom, the epoxy repair compound will last a season if used with care. When removing the wood, it is important to chisel down deep enough to remove all base wax or grundvalla. If some is left, it will boil and eventually break through your new epoxy job when heated by a torch during waxing.

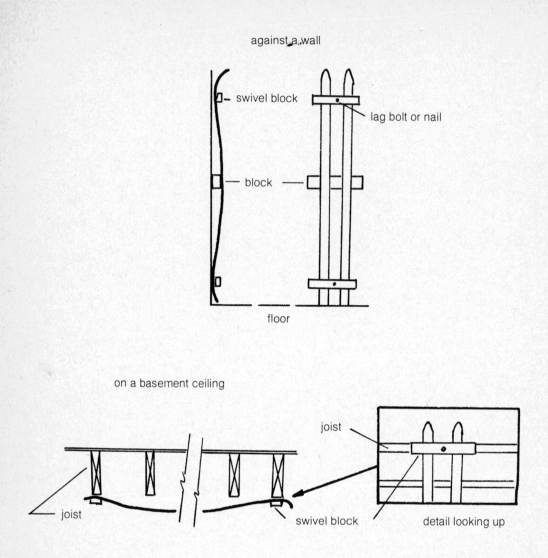

against a wall

swivel block

lag bolt or nail

block

floor

on a basement ceiling

joist

joist

swivel block

detail looking up

Figure 2.6: Ski Storage

Ski Care   Now that you have invested money in getting the best quality, you should protect your investment by caring for your skis. The two main purposes of ski care are to preserve the camber and to prevent warping during that period when the skis are not in use. Skis should not be strapped together in the middle for ex-

tended periods unless they have excessive camber and you are trying to reduce it. When strapped together over the summer, the skis may warp or flatten. If you have not taken care to see that the skis are perfectly matched for stiffness, then one ski is likely to be stiffer and stronger; this ski will act as a press forcing the other ski out of shape. Thus skis should be stored singly and free of confining pressures.

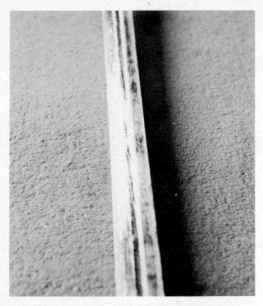

Ski care includes covering bare and worn wood with ground wax

Two effective methods for ski storage are hanging the skis from the floor joists in the basement and mounting them flat against a wall (figure 2.6). In the former case, the skis are allowed to hang by their tips and tails under their own weight; in the latter case the tips and tails are pressed against the wall to hold the skis upright on their tails.

Cross-country skis are susceptible to changes in temperature and moisture conditions, especially as they become older and lose their protective lacquers. Consequently, you should take care to store skis in a cool and relatively dry place (humidity 40 to 60 per cent) over long periods. A very dry storage environment, of course, tends to desiccate the skis, and they become stiffened and less supple. Often though, exposure to snow again will result in reabsorption of lost moisture. On the other hand, you should never leave your skis standing or lying in the snow for extended periods of time. In this situation they will absorb too much moisture and they may warp or the laminations may separate. Extremely cold conditions also put considerable strain on the skis. The cold tends to make the wood and the glue in the ski very brittle, and, as a result, you should not expect too much flexibility from the ski in extremely cold temperatures. In such cases, stand the ski outdoors for fifteen minutes before use and exercise a little caution in bumpy, rough terrain. You will probably avoid a broken ski.

When skis are brought indoors after use, they should be cleaned of snow and ice before being stored even for a few hours. Snow present on the skis usually ends up as a puddle on the floor in which the ski tails are immersed. Invariably the ski tails absorb some of the water, eventually leading to split ski tails. In this respect it is best to stand the skis on their tips with the soles against the wall, so that the tips and not the sliding surfaces of the tails are exposed to possible moisture.

The above suggestions are ways in which you can prolong the structural quality of your skis. Other suggestions on ski care and maintenance will be outlined in the chapter dealing with ski wax and waxing practices, but for the present it is important to realize that cross-country skis are somewhat more fragile and more reactive to heat and moisture than most downhill skis. They do require a little care.

Ski Bindings

In addition to your new skis you will require a binding or harness to attach your boot to the ski—a binding that allows the heel to come up off of the ski. Cross-country ski bindings are many and varied, but all of them allow freedom of movement of the skier's heel; this freedom is essential, as we shall see later, to the technique of cross-country skiing.

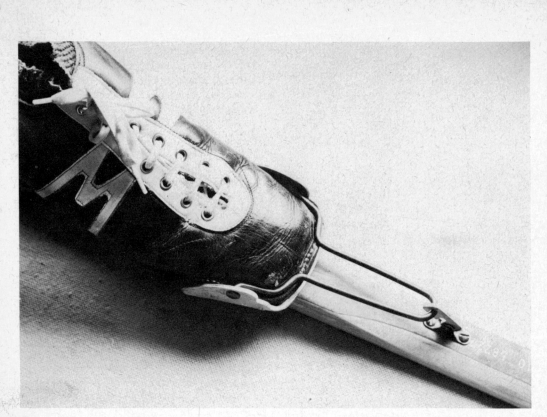

The classical lever harness

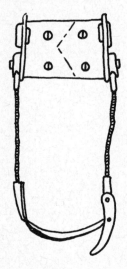

Figure 2.7:   Tempo Binding

Binding Types   A one-time popular touring binding was the Tempo model (figure 2.7), which has a tensioned cable around the heel of the shoe forcing the toe into a solid, box-like toe iron. This binding, although somewhat heavier than other types, is good for touring, in that various shapes and designs of boots can be used with it. In fact older, flexible alpine boots can be used for occasional touring, with a small adjustment of the toe piece. Recently the tempo binding has become more difficult to purchase, for the lightness and freedom of the regular, toe-type bindings has become increasingly more appealing even to rank amateurs. A past misconception equated touring with rather wide, alpine-like skis and converted alpine

The Kloa harness is popular with racers

ski boots. Of course such heavy equipment required a good hefty binding. In such instances the Tempo binding proved best; now, however, people are buying regular, light equipment and finding that the ordinary toe binding, although it looks flimsy, is quite adequate for cross-country tours.

The light, toe type of cross-country ski binding usually requires a properly designed ski boot, because the boot or shoe is held in place by a spring bar that fits onto the somewhat extended sole at the toe of the shoe. Often there are small pins on the surface of the toe piece that protrude up into the shoe sole to prevent the shoe from slipping back out of the harness. Several variations of this type exist and most are acceptable, but there are a few qualities that you should look for in a good binding.

First of all, solid, one-piece bindings are better than the split variety. Split bindings require four or five screws, which increases the chance of splitting the ski. Solid bindings, however, require only three screws and, as a result, are much easier to mount

on the ski. You should also be sure that the pins for holding the boot securely in the harness are fabricated from steel rather than aluminum or white metal. Generally, the softer, white metal pins eventually wear and break, thus rendering the binding useless, even though it may have had very little mileage. Although strength and lightness are the primary criteria in binding selection, don't overlook the ease with which the ski can be put on or removed. In this respect, the Kloa binding is somewhat at a disadvantage, especially for beginners or tourists. Some skiers have experienced difficulty in putting them on, especially in the dark and while wearing pullover, rubber boot-protectors.

For the beginner, then, a good, solid, one-piece aluminum binding with steel pins and a front throw lever is an excellent choice. Don't be taken in by too much gadgetry. Try to select a simple binding, even if it means that you will have to bend over to get it on or off. The main thing is that you will be able to get it to work even in the most adverse conditions.

Assorted ski harnesses or bindings

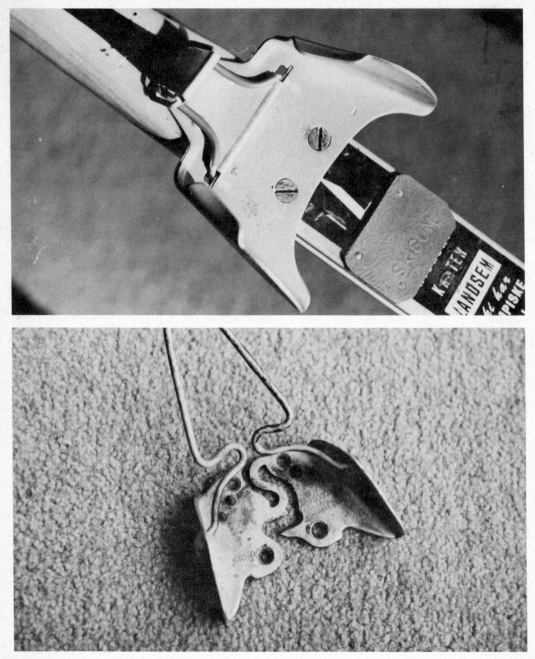

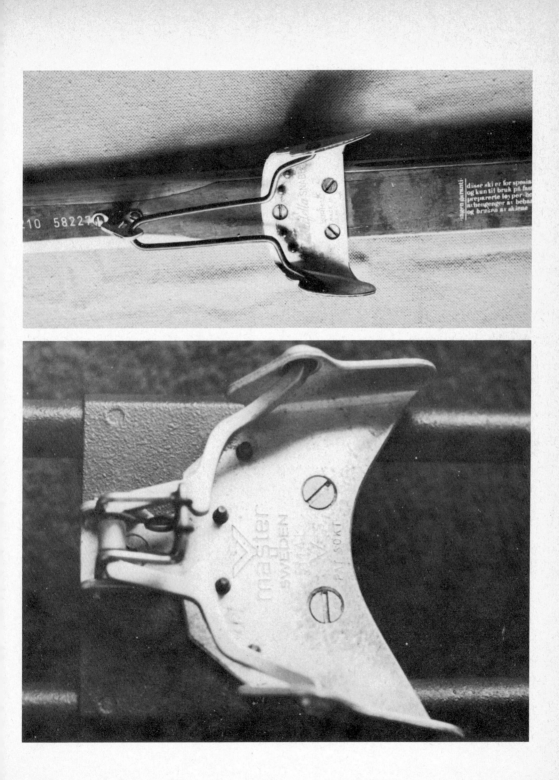

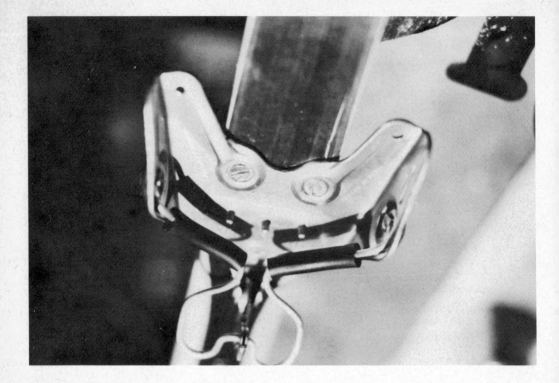

Mounting the Binding Many ski shops charge very high bench fees for the repair or installation of bindings, and, in fact, the fee may be higher than the cost of your cross-country binding itself. In view of this, it is often wise to install or mount your own bindings. There are a few simple rules to follow; essentially the task is a very easy one. First determine the point of balance of the ski by setting it, sole down, on a straight edge on a table, and adjusting it back and forth until the tip and tail rest at an equal height above the plane of the table (figure 2.8). This point on the ski should then be marked with a pencil, and the procedure repeated for the other ski. If a discrepancy exists between the balance points on the two skis, then a mid point between the two marks should be taken as the approximate balance for the pair. The binding is then placed on the skis so that the front-lever sockets on the binding sides are over the balance marks. Mark and drill the front screw hole dead centre on the ski with the harness set for proper balance. Drive the screw in, then insert the boot and adjust the harness sideways so that the boot is straight on the ski. Then gently remove the boot, drill, and drive the two remaining screws.

Holes for screws should be just slightly smaller than the shank of the screw. Use soap on the screws to allow them an easier entry into the wood and to prevent splitting of the ski surface. Although oil or grease will also serve as lubricants, they are not recommended, in that oil tends to remain in the wood and weaken the fibres. If you make a mistake in drilling, or wish to change the binding position, don't panic.

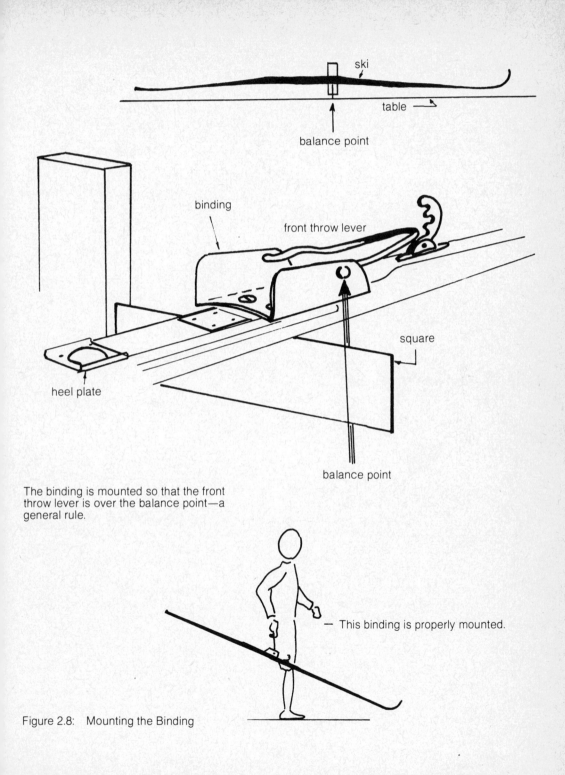

ski

table

balance point

binding

front throw lever

square

heel plate

balance point

The binding is mounted so that the front throw lever is over the balance point—a general rule.

— This binding is properly mounted.

Figure 2.8:   Mounting the Binding

The misplaced holes can be plugged by shaving a stick of wood to size and tapping it lightly into the screw hole, filled with waterproof glue. It is imperative to plug all holes, not only to restore strength to the wood in the area of the screw hole, but also to prevent water from entering the ski.

Again put the ski boot in its operational position; press the front lever down onto the rim of the sole to press the binding pegs into the sole. Add a little pencil lead to the pegs beforehand to ensure that you will see the peg impressions on the boot sole clearly. The making of the holes to accommodate the pegs is discussed in the next section on boots. If the skis are of good quality and balance and the binding mounted properly, then the ski tips will hang down at angles of from 40 to 60 degrees when the skis are held by the front levers (figure 2.8). With experience, a skier can adjust the bindings behind or ahead of the balance point to suit his preference for either heavy or light tips respectively. With a heavy tip the ski will tend to follow in the track much easier at the finish of the kick but, on the other hand, will be somewhat more difficult to turn.

Binding Adjustments   Certain minor adjustments can be made to the bindings. If the toe of the boot pinches on the side of the binding when it is bent upward then the binding can be spread slightly by bending the side plates with pliers or a hammer. Occasionally the front levers are not curved sufficiently to cover enough of the lip of the sole at the front of the boot to obtain a good grip to hold it stable. In such a case it is possible to shape the front lever to the boot by heating sections of it with a propane torch until red and then bending it with pliers for a better fit. One word of advice here, and that is that you should try to get the proper binding for the proper boot. Most boots are shaped to fit most

cross-country bindings, but there are some combinations that may give some problems. The Karhu boot, an extremely good, sturdy boot, fits best in the binding of the same name, although, with a minor amount of shoving and jogging, it can be made to fit other bindings such as the Roteffella "Snabb" and "Gull" models. When buying, be sure to check in the store, or ask someone who is using the same brand, how well the boots and bindings fit.

Binding sizes come in two or three groups and are made to fit various sized boots. Usually there are two binding sizes, small and large; the small binding fits boots up to size 43 and the large fits sizes over 43. There may also be a third size, medium, which fits somewhere between size 30 and 43 boots. Even though these sizes are fairly consistent, it is best if you have no experience to try the fit before you buy.

Heel Plates   Included with the bindings are heel plates, which serve two purposes. One, they should prevent snow from building up under the heel in wet conditions, and two, they should provide more lateral control on corners and downhills. Rubber and metal heel plates have proved most popular and efficient, although some metal ones are shaped in such a way as to collect snow under certain conditions. Often it is wise to put some type of rubber beneath the ball of the foot just behind the binding, because snow tends to collect there, particularly when the lacquered ski finish begins to wear and the wood is exposed. Once the exposed wood becomes damp, snow and ice accumulate rapidly, to the annoyance of the skier. Some skis have a very durable and high-quality finish and thus do not require pads or plates, but through trial and error you will find that heel plates are more comfortable and they don't cost much anyway.

Heel plates: typical rubber (top) and metal (bottom) models

Ski boots: (left to right) racing, light touring, heavy touring, and alpine

Boots

Because the cross-country skier seeks out bush trails and variable terrain to slide along, he requires great freedom in his ankles. In cross-country skiing and touring the snow is usually soft, and turning is accomplished by stepping or skating from one foot to the other. Cross-country boots then should be like soft, leather shoes, attached to the ski only at the toe by a light aluminum harness, giving maximum freedom of the heel, and allowing the skier to come up on his toes at the completion of each step much in the same manner as when walking.

Recently, with advances in the technology of synthetic materials, boot soles have been made from vinyl, which seems thus far to be very satisfactory. Problems were encountered with earlier plastic and rubber soles, for in cold weather such materials tended to become brittle and break. Other variations have leather as the basic structural element, but also have a thin veneer of vinyl or rubber on the sole as a waterproofing agent. Even so, with prolonged use these veneers will sometimes crack. Try to

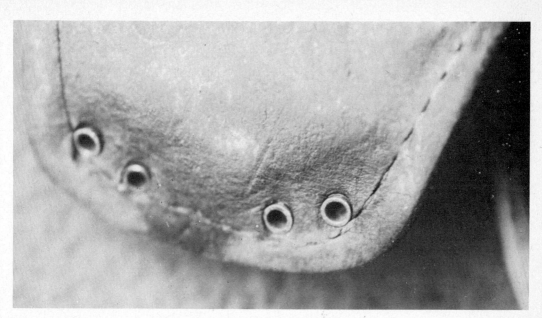

Brass ferrules to protect the boot sole
from the binding pins

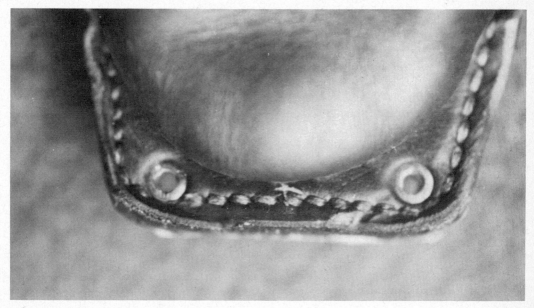

The Kloa binding requires brass ferrules
through the lip of the boot

choose the boot having either a totally leather sole or a very thin veneer of rubber or plastic. One would think that a thicker veneer should last longer but because it is thicker it tends to be less flexible and breaks more easily than the thinner veneers.

Boot Care   Leather cross-country ski boots require the same care and maintenance as any leather shoe. Constant subjection to alternating wet and dry conditions often makes the leather stiff and hard to bend. Leather soles and uppers should be softened by applying either linseed oil or a commercial boot wax. This will prevent wet feet and also keep blisters and sore spots from developing on the foot due to abrasive, dry leather. New boots are particularly abrasive on toes and heels until they soften. If the skier's heel is affected, often it is possible to remove the hard, fibre heel cup from the boot, leaving only the softer, outer leather against the heel. Although this practice removes some strength from the boot, it does alleviate the pressure on blistered heels and still leaves the ski boot in usable condition.

Caution should be exercised when drying boots. Don't set them on a very hot radiator to dry because they will become as hard as rock and no amount of cursing or condemnation will allow entry into the boots. It is better to stand the boot upright with the toe on the floor and the heel against the side of the radiator, and the laces loosened, so that moisture can escape slowly upward, leaving the boot still relatively soft.

Binding Holes   As mentioned earlier, most bindings or harnesses require holes in the soles of the boots to accommodate the pins that prevent the boots from slipping backwards out of the binding. These holes may present some problems in terms of their drilling and maintenance. The positions of the holes are determined by placing the boot in the binding, aligning the boot on the ski so that the centre of the heel is on the centre of the ski, and pressing the front lever down on the front lip of the sole. Holes are then made in the sole at the imprints made by the pins either by hand drilling them or burning them with a hot nail or coat hanger. Many skiers prefer to burn the holes, because it seems to harden the leather and make the holes more durable. Often when the boot soles become wet the holes tend to enlarge, as the leather stretches and excessive lateral movement of the boot in the binding results. You can prevent this condition by installing commercially available brass ferrules in the holes when you first drill them. Although they provide good stability, some skiers dislike the ferrules because they come out of the sole when it becomes dried out. Experience has shown that if the leather sole is periodically rubbed with linseed oil around the ferrules, they will remain intact for the life of the boot. The leather tends to swell slightly when impregnated with linseed oil, resulting in a tight grip on the ferrules. This will work even with rubber-veneered boots, if the oil is placed into the ferrule and allowed to seep through the hole in its end. Other reinforcing devices such as metal plates are available and are suitable for touring equipment, but are usually too heavy for competition equipment. Some boots come with manufactured holes for binding pins. Be sure that the boot holes match the harness pins when you buy.

Boot Sizes   Boot sizes are normally given in European sizes. A convenient table is given here with conversions to North American sizes.

Table 2.4 Boot Sizes

Women	Men Children	European Equivalent
	1	33
	2	34
	2½ - 3	35
	3½	36
5½ - 6	4 - 4½	37
6½	5	38
7 - 7½	5½ - 6	39
8	6½	40
8½ - 9	7 - 7½	41
9½	8	42
10	9	43
	9½ - 10	44
	10½	45
	11 - 11½	46
	12	47

Ski Poles

The next item of equipment to be introduced is the ski pole, which, again, should be light, relatively flexible, and strong. Often deep snow conditions are encountered along the trail, so the cross-country pole is longer than the alpine pole. In cross-country skiing the pole is used much more than in alpine skiing. It acts as a support to maintain the lateral balance of the skier. It acts as a means of propulsion to push the skier over the snow and as both a means of support and propulsion while climbing hills. A good cross-country ski pole will be somewhat flexible and springy, so that it provides a good snap when used for propelling the skier forward on the trail.

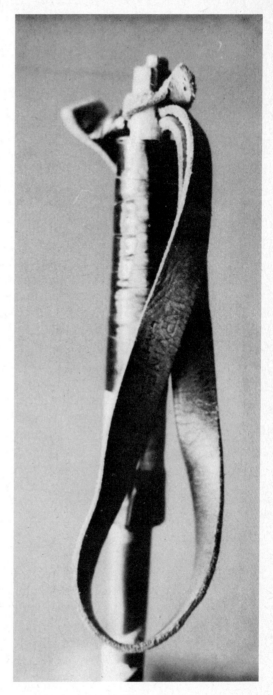

The "Finnish" handle

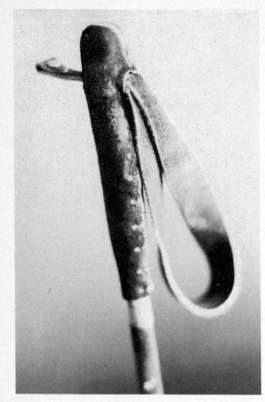

The "Norwegian" handle

Construction   Until recently, cross-country ski poles were traditionally made from treated cane or bamboo, which provided, in addition to strength, a reasonably flexible shaft, to provide an extra push, much in the same way that the fibreglass vaulting pole adds momentum to a pole vaulter's leap. For this reason the stiffer alpine ski poles are not often used by cross-country ski buffs.

Within the past five years fibreglass and light aluminum and steel alloys have begun to surpass cane and bamboo as ski pole shaft material. Most of these materials tend to be lighter and stronger than cane and they require less maintenance. The best glass poles are those constructed of spirally spun fibreglass tubes of fairly constant diameter. Although a great number of expert skiers use them, the poles have been known to shatter on cold days, when banged inadvertently together or against a tree. Consequently, the steel and aluminum alloys seem to be becoming more popular, particularly among the competitive group of skiers.

There are many varieties of cross-country ski poles on the market now. Much of the variation in poles occurs in the baskets (the rings on the bottom) and in the handles. Some of the many varieties are represented in the accompanying photographs. The older Finnish-type handle was quite popular on cane poles, and offered a simple strap adjustment, but now most poles employ the newer, more compact strap, as seen to the left. Ski pole baskets now are invariably plastic. Most are fairly durable, but in selecting a basket try to get one that has flexible webbing. Stiff webbing has a tendency to cause the ski pole to slip or pop out of the snow on the backward arm extension so that the skier can't put all his force into the push.

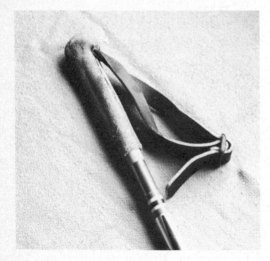

A common adjustable strap type

Ski Pole Length   Suggested ski pole lengths were given earlier, in table 2.3. They increase in length from 90 cm to 160 cm by 5 cm increments, but half sizes, such as 142.5 cm, for example, can also be obtained.

A general rule is that poles are of proper length if they come up under the armpits when the pole tip is rested on the ski surface. Personal preference and the terrain will govern whether you will require a slightly shorter or longer ski pole. On a very hilly trail with steep climbs, often it is advisable to use a shorter pole, which tends to draw you closer to the snow and forces a desired, deeply bent knee while running uphill. As well, you do not have to reach so far ahead while climbing in order to get a good purchase on the snow with the shorter pole, and it will not slip back or pop out of the snow on steep uphills so readily as a longer pole. Conversely, where a trail is composed of primarily flat or gently rolling terrain, a longer pole is better, to accommodate the more upright body position encountered in the diagonal and double pole strides. Many ski poles have adjustable handstraps, which allow you effectively to adjust the length of your poles. By lengthening the handstrap, you grasp the handle lower on the shaft, thus shortening your effective pole length. On the other hand, through shortening the handstrap, you really grasp the pole higher on the shaft and thus lengthen the effective pole length. In this manner, you can adjust one pair of poles as much as two inches to suit differing conditions. If more length adjustment is required, then the poles can be cut, but keep in mind some of the following hints.

Ski Pole Adjustments   Adjustments that can be made to ski poles are confined mainly to handstraps, length, and tips. Ski

The "Finnish" basket

A modern, plastic, pre-slanted basket

pole length can be altered by removing the handles and cutting off a section. Generally it is unadvisable to cut the lower end of the pole, as this will shorten the solid core into which the tip is usually inserted, and there is a chance that the thread on the tip may protrude through the core into the hollow shaft, weakening the purchase. Of course, metal poles are usually tapered toward the tip and cannot be cut without destroying the balance of the pole, but old, Finnish-type poles with a hole drilled through the cane just above the handle to accommodate the handstrap must be shortened by cutting a length from the bottom end. Experience has shown that it is easier to tap extra filler lightly into the bottom to hold the threads of the metal tip than it is to try to drill a new hole at the top for the handle strap. Bamboo and cane are very difficult to drill unless confined in a metal sheath or some such device to prevent splitting. When replacing the handles on your poles, be sure to put some glue on their inner surfaces to ensure a good tight fit; as well, renew the rivets. Nothing is more annoying than to lose your pole handle five or ten miles from home or the car. Most glues are useless for metal or leather, but the slow-drying epoxy glues in small tubes have become the universal fix-all for cross-country skiers in repairing ski poles, boots, and skis.

Some steel poles have a tendency to pop out of the snow prematurely during the finishing phase of diagonal poling, especially on uphills, thus denying the skier the full benefit of his pole thrust. Assuming proper length and a flexible basket, the other possible reason for this phenomenon is that the section of shaft below the basket is too straight. This problem can be remedied by heating the shaft just below the basket until it is red hot and lightly tapping

The basic ski outfit

it with a hammer to bend it toward the front of the pole (i.e., the face of the pole opposite to the handstrap). New models of light alloy have this feature already built in.

Wax

Finally, you will need some ski wax. Cross-country ski wax has special properties, in that the same wax allows you both to climb straight up hills and to shuss down the other side. It is a very versatile substance, but you will find that variations in snow conditions and temperature will demand variations in wax type. Thus, you will require a few different types to be able to accommodate most touring trail conditions.

In Chapter 4 on waxing, a more detailed discussion will reveal the techniques of waxing as well as the subtle variations in quality of the various brands.

Clothing and Fancy Stuff

It is not necessary to purchase cross-country ski clothing if you are just a beginner. Thus, your initial capital outlay can be shaved by a substantial amount. As in most sports, special clothing is really superfluous and generally is marked up to exorbitant prices. Although we won't go so far as to call them "Aunt Mabel's old-time gym bloomers", an old, baggy pair of pants stuffed into the tops of some work socks and underlined by underwear provide a suitable garb for the lower body. Couple these with a fishnet undershirt, a turtleneck jersey, and a woollen sweater and you have a very functional touring outfit. A pair of lined leather mitts, or even a pair of woollen gloves, and a woollen toque complete the essentials. A word of caution though: always overdress. If you have extra clothes on, you can take them off if you find

The basic outfit — underwear, toque,
turtleneck, knee socks, gloves, and nylon
knickers and top

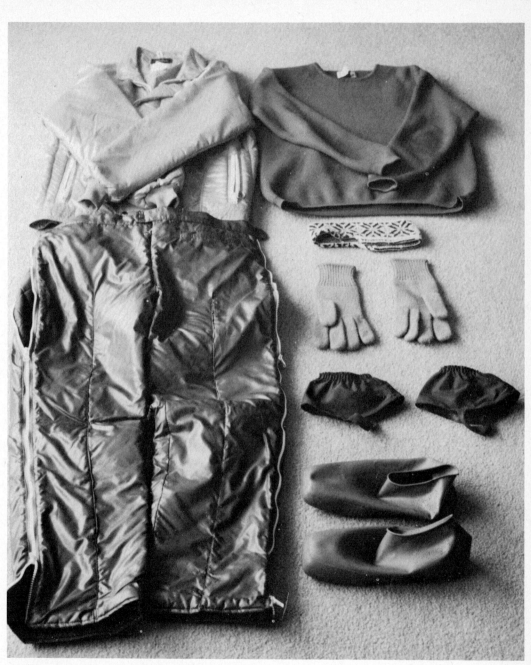

*Additional clothing for extreme weather— nylon
jacket, warm-up pants, sweater, headband,
mittens, spats, and rubber-boot pullovers*

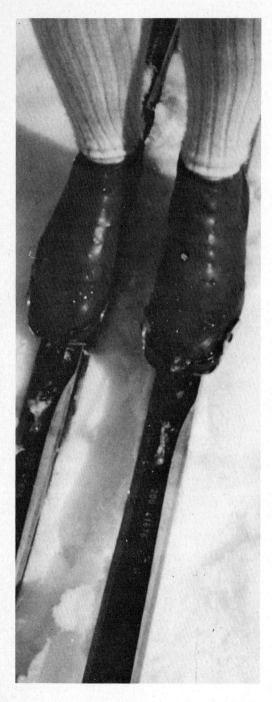

the going too hot, but if you begin to get cold in late afternoon as the sun begins to drop towards the horizon, you may wish that you had that extra sweater or light jacket to break the chill. During heavy going in rough terrain or in the bright spring sun, you will often find sweat trickling down your face and back, but once you stop you will be even more prone to the cold. Take no chances and bring extra clothing in a small pack if you plan to stop for lunch or a rendezvous. Of course, if you are in a hurry and expect to push right on without any stops, your continued body motion will keep you plenty warm, providing that you don't become completely exhausted.

Later, when funds and interest permit, you can invest in a ski suit, knicker socks, and gloves. Such suits are usually made from stretch nylon and are very durable. lasting up to ten years with continual use or even longer with occasional use. Most suits are made in Scandinavia and come in a variety of colours and styles. The two-piece style is the most popular, with the one-piece suit being more popular with the racing fraternity. As with other sports, cross-country skiing is not without its fashionable items and most of these suits have the usual stripes and designs to attract the eye and empty the pocketbook.

Several other fancy items, which are not really necessary but which you may find useful, are gaiters or spats, rubber-boot pullovers, cross-country ski gloves, and warm-up suits. Gaiters are a useful item if you plan to do a lot of off-track skiing in deep snow. They are somewhat akin to a cuff that covers the top of the boot to prevent snow from getting into the boot. Rubber-boot pullovers are very handy in the spring or during wet, sloppy ski

For extremely cold conditions, rubber-boot pullovers are a boon

conditions. The pullover is a soft, stretchy rubber that fits over the whole boot, thus protecting it from water and keeping the skier's feet dry. In the 1968 Winter Olympics many skiers used them to race in during a very warm spell at Grenoble, France. Cross-country ski gloves are especially designed to allow air to circulate around the back of the hand. They have leather palms with cotton netted backs and are very comfortable to wear. In cold weather, though, many people find them rather flimsy protection and revert to woollen or lined leather gloves. The cross-country ski gloves are particularly cold after you have been skiing and have stopped. The hands, dampened with sweat, are quick to freeze up, so if you get a pair of these gloves you won't be able to do much else but ski in them.

CHAPTER 3

The Cross-Country Ski Technique

Basically, anyone who can walk can ski cross-country over the easiest terrain. One of the beauties of the sport is that you can begin immediately to make full use of your equipment without lessons or the need for learning any special skills. Moreover, safety need not be a major concern at this stage, as it is highly unlikely that you will injure yourself in such light, flexible equipment on flat terrain.

The first step in obtaining freedom on your skis is to lace up and get out onto a snow-covered football field or park. Try some easy shuffling along. Place one foot ahead of the other and essentially walk on your skis. In this manner you will soon develop a feel for your equipment and the balance required to negotiate the ground on skis. Undoubtedly the first few outings will be a little shaky and you will rely a great deal on your poles for balance and support, but if you persist, soon you should be able to shuffle across the fields with short, sliding steps, quite easily and naturally.

The first few outings will necessarily produce some fatigue, unless you are a well-trained athlete. Maintaining balance and trying to carry out the unfamiliar technical moves of skiing bring premature fatigue, not a sore, unpleasant fatigue, but a mild sense of exhilaration, a mild exhaustion of the whole body, which allows you to relax completely and without guilt in an armchair before the fire.

The big difference between the faltering steps of the beginner and the long, easy stride of the experienced skier, relaxed and confident mile after mile, is technique. In cross-country skiing the purpose of your efforts is to move forward across the snow with minimum effort. The snow really presents a resistance to your motion as well as providing a slippery surface over which your skis will slide. Technique is needed to make maximum use of these aspects and to minimize lateral motion and backslip.

Now that you have selected your equipment, the next step is to learn how to use it. This aspect of cross-country skiing—learning and mastering the various movements used to traverse the countryside on skis—is known as "technique". The basic motion involved is quite similar to walking, and is known in cross-country jargon as "the stride". It incorporates a kick-glide sequence of the legs and skis over the snow.

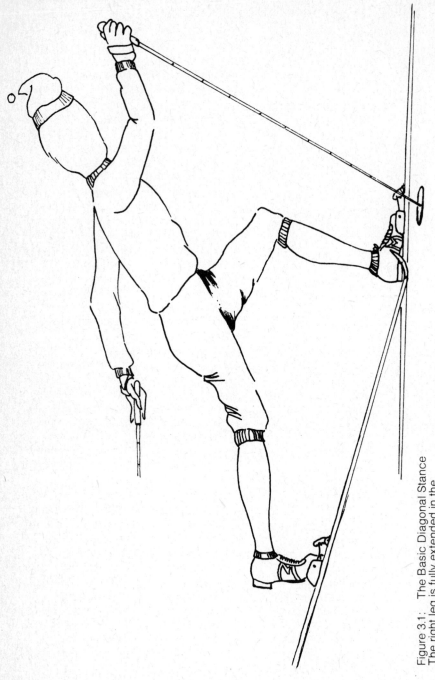

Figure 3.1: The Basic Diagonal Stance The right leg is fully extended in the follow-through of the kick. The left leg supports the skier's weight during the glide. The right pole is planted into the snow opposite the left foot by a slightly crooked arm. The left pole is forced up and to the rear by the follow-through of the pole push.

By alternately pushing each ski downwards and backwards on the snow and gliding on the opposing one, the skier effectively moves forward in the track. Thus, the underlying principle of the cross-country ski technique is that a backward kick produces a forward glide.

The Diagonal Stride

The motions of the basic technique, the diagonal stride, are very simple to grasp, in that they are similar to a brisk walking or skating motion. One leg provides the forward thrust by kicking down onto the snow and following through to the rear, while the other leg provides a pedestal for the skier's weight under which the ski glides smoothly forward. Simultaneously, the arms swing naturally in opposing frequency just as if one were marching along the trail. The resulting motion is a smooth rhythmical alternation of the upper and lower limbs from a kicking position to a gliding position (see figure 3.1).

Notice that the initial downward thrust of the forward leg is critical for gaining a solid bond between that ski and the snow. Without this "planting action", the forward ski may not grip the snow well enough and it will slip back when you attempt to push off it.

Important too is the complete shift of weight from one foot to the other, so that at the end of the kick (the down and back motion of the forward leg), the weight is carried entirely by the opposing leg, which is then gliding in the forward position itself, ready to kick down and back. All of the motion oscillates from one foot and arm to the other and thus from one ski to the other, hence the name, diagonal stride. When the weight is transferred to the gliding ski, it not only facilitates the slide by increasing the inertia of that ski, but also provides a greater downward force to aid the wax in gripping the snow for the next kick.

To understand the principles behind the basic ski stride, study carefully figure 3.1 and the following discussion of leg and arm motions.

Leg Motion   Identify the kicking and gliding skis of the skier in figure 3.1. The skier has brought the stride to full extension or to the end of the kick. The gliding (left) ski is flat on the snow, supporting the skier's weight, and the kicking (right) ski is raised above the snow to the rear by the follow-through of the thrust of the kick. Note that the heel of the boot has come up off the ski as a result of this backward extension, demonstrating the need for light and flexible boots. Working from the skis upward, the basic technique can be appreciated from a discussion of the following details in figure 3.1.

First, the position of the right ski at the culmination of the kick indicates the force and direction of the rearward thrust. The tail of the kicking ski has left the surface of the snow as a result of the continuing momentum of the rearward thrust. In an effort to emulate the kick, beginners often lift their ski tails off the snow by bending the knee during the rearward motion of the leg. This action tends to cut off the kick too early, resulting both in a loss of timing with the arms and a loss of power in the kick, and it should be avoided. Try to let your kicking leg extend rearward in a natural, easy fashion. The tip of the kicking ski remains on the snow opposite the gliding foot so that the toe of the boot can be used to give it direction or to keep it in the track. The gliding (left) ski is flat and is supporting the weight of the skier.

The kicking leg has been fully extended to the rear in a relatively straight line, but it is not locked at the knee. If the knee is still bent at the finish of your kick or the leg is

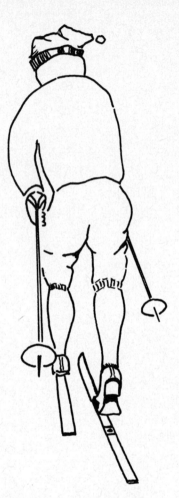

Figure 3.2: Front and Rear View of the Diagonal Stride

not properly extended, then the thrust of the kick has been incomplete or weak. In such a case you are not gaining the full benefit of your leg work and you are practising poor technique. The return of the kicking leg and ski to the glide position is relaxed and pendulum-like, requiring very little energy. No attempt should be made to kick this ski forward into the gliding position. The only motion that is forced in the leg work of the cross-country ski technique is the powerful rearward kick.

Another detail that can also be appreciated from figure 3.1 is that the gliding leg has been bent to a position where the knee lies just above the toe of the gliding foot. If the knee is in front of the toe of the gliding boot, then the leg has been bent too deeply and energy is being wasted in trying to keep the knees so deeply bent. On the other hand, if the knee rests above and behind the boot, then energy will be wasted in pulling the foot back behind the knee to a position where it can begin to press down for the kick. In summation then, the knee of the gliding foot should be bent to a comfortable angle where the skier's weight can be brought into play immediately for the subsequent kick.

Arm Motion   The arm motion associated with the basic diagonal is a natural rhythmic swing and push motion in opposing phase to the leg motion. For example, when the right leg is extended in the kick phase the opposing left arm is also at full extension to the rear in the follow through from the push with the ski pole. Conversely, the right arm is extended forward to plant the ski pole into the snow in a position suitable for the beginning of the next arm push and leg kick.

Although the position of the arms is rather important, you should not try consciously to achieve the proper position at first. Instead, try to develop a natural swing of the arms that feels fluid and comfortable. Once you have mastered this motion, you can then concentrate on developing a purposeful arm action to benefit your stride.

The change over from the swing of the arms during walking to a swing suitable for skiing is relatively simple, with the only significant difference being in the increased amount of extension forward and to the rear. In skiing, the pushing arm (the left arm in figure 3.1) is extended entirely backward, with a fast, if not violent, flick of the wrist, but not so hard as to lock the elbow. During this rearward push the arm and ski pole should be kept as close as possible to the body in order to keep the arms pushing straight back and not to the side. The hand

should follow a curved path from a position slightly in over the ski in front of the body, around the thighs to a position behind the small of the back.

If you experience some difficulty in timing your arms and legs, try a small diversion. Hold your ski poles in the middle and balance them in each hand so they are parallel to the snow surface. Then stride off on your skis and swing your arms (still balancing the poles) back and forth with the frequency of your striding. This little exercise will soon provide you with a rhythmical coordination of your upper and lower body. Soon your mind will forget the arms, and they will swing and push naturally with the motion of the legs.

In analyzing figure 3.1 further, you will note that the right arm, while reaching forward to plant the ski pole, is not extended fully to a point where the elbow is locked. Instead it is crooked slightly at the elbow, in order that the pole can be planted in the snow opposite the gliding (left) foot. If your leading arm (right) is too straight at the elbow, you might tend to plant the ski pole too far forward, and as a result you will have to draw yourself forward to the pole before you can push with it. Therefore, the arm must be bent enough to allow the pole to be planted opposite the gliding foot where you can immediately apply the strength of your shoulders and arms to push on the pole. With too little forward extension there is also the danger of not reaching forward far enough, in which case you will plant your ski pole too early, before the finish of the kick of your opposite leg. This error has a tendency to hurry the termination of the kick, resulting in the incomplete extension of the kicking leg and loss of power in the kick. By the time you have put the pole into the snow and tried to use it, you will have slid past the point where you can push on it.

The ski pole should not be gripped tightly

in the hand. On the forward swing the fingers are loosely wrapped around the handle of the pole and on the backward extension the pole is held loosely between the thumb and forefinger (figure 3.4). During the thrust phase of poling, the grip may tighten slightly, but the major part of the push is taken by the pole handle straps, which in turn transfer it to the pole shaft, propelling you forward. A tightly gripped pole will tire and perhaps cramp the arm muscles; at the same time it reduces the general efficiency of the arm motion. Thus a relaxed grip of the ski poles is important to both rhythm and strength in the extensive use of a good technique.

Muscle Groups   With practice the kick-glide sequence is done as subconsciously as one might push off on skates or sustain a brisk walk. Further details of cross-country ski technique can be appreciated by the examination of the sequence of actions of the various muscle groups employed. Assume that a stride is at completion, as in figure 3.1.

In the instant that the weight is transferred to the gliding leg (left), the knee assumes a position to "plant" the ski onto

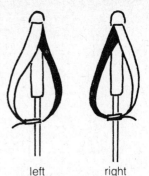

left   right

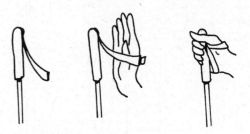

Figure 3.3   Gripping the Ski Pole
Put your hand up through the loop, then grip the handle. The lower strap should be on the thumb side of the grip.

Figure 3.4:   Ski-pole grip during the diagonal

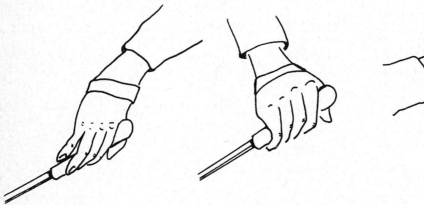

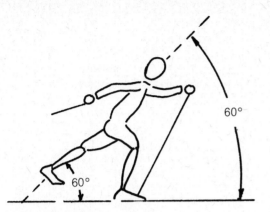

60°

60°

Figure 3.5:   Body Position

the snow to make the wax grip for the subsequent kick. With the flexing of this knee, the powerful hip muscles, aided by the body weight, begin the motion of the kick. The hips are a large, strong muscle group and have the power to overcome the static friction between the ski and the snow. At the same time the powerful shoulder muscles, also aided by body weight, begin to push on the opposite ski pole. As the ski begins to glide, its lesser kinetic friction is easily overcome by the relatively weaker calf and lower leg muscles, along with the triceps in the opposing arm. While the kick travels down the leg into the ankle, the forward speed increases, eventually reaching a maximum for push by leg and arm. At this time a quick flick of the ankle and wrist provide the final acceleration and add effectively to the speed. The ankle and the wrist are not exceptionally strong, compared to the thigh or shoulder, but they can, because of their quickness, add to the speed generated by the kick. Although the motion of the kick begins in the slower, more powerful muscle groups, do not think of the kick as a slow or relaxed motion. On the contrary, it is the quick, explosive part of the stride and is directed totally behind the skier. This aspect is particularly impor-

tant to would-be competitors; European coaches have remarked in the past concerning North American racers, that the lack of this explosive kick is their main failing.

Body Position   How does one know if he is in fact doing the right thing? In the beginning it is difficult to assess your own progress, because it is difficult to extricate yourself from the process. Your mind is often concentrating on the track ahead and is not necessarily free to focus on what your legs or arms are doing. At this stage it is best to seek an observer's opinion (provided of course that he knows something about cross-country skiing), because he can objectively look for clues as to the efficiency of your technique. Apart from a complete arm and leg extension, the best clue is the over-all body position. At the completion of the kick, the head and kicking leg should lie in a relatively straight line having an angle of from fifty to sixty degrees to the horizontal (figure 3.5). Again, do not try to attain this position *per se.* Try to execute the proper kick and glide, and if everything is correct and complete, then this straight line relationship should appear automatically. With the head in line with the body, your eyes should seek a point from twenty to thirty feet ahead on the track, where they can interpret the upcoming terrain. Staring directly down at the ski tips may produce tension in your neck and shoulders as well as destroying the efficiency of your body position for the kick.

Summary   In learning to ski there is no substitute for practice. All of the written words on the technique and terminology of cross-country skiing are no match for getting out on the snow with your cross-country outfit and becoming involved with the new sensations and feelings offered by this winter mode of travel. Once you have gained your balance, the weight shift from the kicking to the gliding ski will likely be intuitive. Having co-ordinated the movements of your arms and legs through frequent use of your equipment, you will soon "feel" the need for a full extension of the leg and arm in the push phase and so on. Then you can return to the written word and pick up the finer points if you wish.

The role of experience and practice in improving technique has been demonstrated over and over again by the Scandinavian racing heroes. Their philosophy is that, eventually, when you have skied far enough, perhaps 4,000 kilometres (2,500 miles), you will develop an efficient and tireless technique that is uniquely suited to your own body strength and proportion. Perhaps the philosophy now is more suited to leisure skiing than to competition, where mere hundredths of a second can separate gold from silver and where precision and discipline are playing ever-increasing roles. Nevertheless, the philosophy is basically sound—the more skiing that you do, the better you will ski.

Putting it all together then, the result is a free-moving kick-glide sequence with alternating rhythms of work during the kick and rest during the glide phases. Even though the motion appears to be lethargic and relaxed, the kick must be a quick, snappy, hard, downward then rearward thrust to get maximum forward glide. This is the diagonal stride and the result of putting together several strides, as seen in figure 3.6, is known as cross-country skiing.

Advanced Technique

The foregoing discussion has been essentially a clinical presentation of the basic cross-country technique, the diagonal stride. Through practice, the occasional skier or tourer can develop the diagonal stride into a smoothly flowing kick-glide sequence, which he will find thoroughly adequate for negotiating fields and wood lots. For the more serious skier, or the racer, however, the sustained use of the diagonal stride may be tiring or boring or inadequate in certain terrain. As a result, various modifications have been developed to alleviate the fatigue of the constant poling required in the diagonal stride and to accommodate the usual variations in terrain. Some top racers favour the diagonal throughout a race, broken only by a double pole stride in faster sections of the track, but the majority of cross-country ski racers favour variety and employ the following

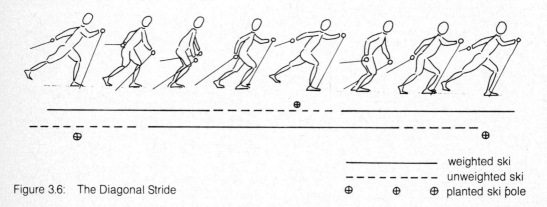

	weighted ski
- - - - - - - -	unweighted ski
⊕ ⊕ ⊕	planted ski pole

Figure 3.6:   The Diagonal Stride

The perfect diagonal stride

variations of the diagonal in advantageous situations of terrain, either to rest or to increase their speed. In racing, of course, the primary concern is speed, and a thorough familiarity with all of the variations is essential.

In touring you can use the variations to relieve fatigue in the arms and shoulders or to navigate around obstacles along the trail. In order to employ the variations to advantage, you should practise until the transition from one to the other is smooth,

unbroken, and rhythmical. Do not become preoccupied with the variations, however, until you have mastered a good, sound diagonal technique first.

The Three-Step Diagonal   The main variations of the diagonal stride are the three-step (often called the passgang or change-up) and the four-step diagonal strides. These variations give the arms and shoulders a rest and relax tired breathing muscles in the chest. The three-step diagonal, as the name suggests, involves

Figure 3.7:   The Three-Step Diagonal

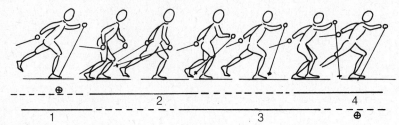

Figure 3.8:   The Four-Step Diagonal

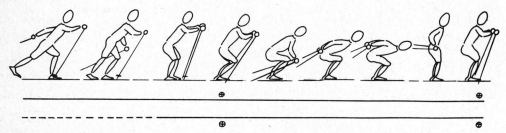

Figure 3.9:   The Double Pole

three steps from one pole push to the next one (figure 3.7). The rhythm may be somewhat difficult to grasp at first, so it is best to start with the diagonal stride and work from there into the three-step variation. When the change is made from a straight diagonal stride, the right arm swings forward slowly so that the pole hangs free of the ground, while the left leg begins to press and kick back. Meanwhile, the left pole is brought forward and planted in the snow at the termination of the kick of the left foot. Then the right leg begins the next kick, at the end of which the right pole, having rested for three complete kicks or steps, comes into play again. Essentially, all that has happened is that the right ski pole has missed one push while the left pole has continued in sequence with the leg motion —the basic diagonal. In this manner both arms can be rested by alternating the three-step diagonal from side to side.

The Four-Step Diagonal   In the four-step diagonal stride (figure 3.8), the right ski pole swings even more slowly forward, resting the arm for four steps in this case. The pole is planted into the snow immediately at the termination of the fourth kick (that of the right leg in figure 3.8). Thus, in the four-step diagonal stride the arms are poling at half the rate at which the legs are striding, and the work load of the arms and shoulders is temporarily reduced. The kick and arm actions are identical to those in the basic diagonal kick-glide sequence, except when the arm is planted at the end of the fourth step. At this point the right shoulder drops the skier's weight onto the ski pole emphatically, to give the pole a quick snap to the rear, and as a result, the upper body rebounds to an almost upright position, allowing for a forced opening of the chest and lungs as well as an increase in speed.

You should not concentrate on proper. body, arm, and leg positions when first attempting the diagonal variations. You should just allow them to materialize naturally out of the rhythm of the diagonal stride itself. Only a small initiating movement is required to change from the basic diagonal to a three-step modification. Simply allow one of your arms to remain in a forward and upward position while carrying out the basic diagonal movements with the other arm and the legs. This procedure will soon have you executing change-ups without thinking at all of how and where your arms and legs are functioning. For the four-step variation you simply slow the frequency of your arm movements relative to those of your legs, but maintain the same motion as in the basic diagonal.

The Double Pole   The double pole stride, usually referred to as the "double pole", is really unrelated to the basic diagonal stride, in that both arms are used to push simultaneously and the legs do not kick, as illustrated in figure 3.9.

From the diagonal stride a smooth change into a double pole stance is made by drawing the kicking leg forward and parallel to the gliding leg and by extending both arms forward from the body in the glide phase. Then the skier's weight is transferred to the balls of the feet and the knees are dropped at the same instant as the poles are planted. Although the poles are planted somewhat farther ahead of the foot than in the diagonal stride, the arms do not begin to push until the feet have glided forward adjacent to the poles. When the poles are in a position to push back, the arms bend at the elbows, so that the body weight "hangs" on the poles for an instant as the knees are dropped or bent. In this manner the skier can get some free momentum by allowing gravity to weight his poles and begin the backward thrust. Subsequent to the weighting of the poles, the shoulders apply their strength, first to pull the body forward, then to begin the push to the rear. Simultaneously, the body begins to bend forward at the midsection, bringing the stomach muscles into play. As the arms pass close to the thighs and are fully extended to the rear, they naturally rise up and inward in a follow-through from the force of the push. A quick flick of the wrist just when the pole is about to leave the snow will further accelerate the speed of the double pole. A complete rearward extension of the arms in the double pole stride is essential in order to gain the maximum push from the arm work. Beginners are tempted to terminate the arm push at the thighs, and a significant loss of momentum results. This rather explosive follow-through also tends to throw the upper body into a forward and upright position, where the chest is relaxed for easier breathing during the short glide phase before the next double pole.

A few further aspects of the double pole stride can be appreciated by examining the position of the body over the skis. At the beginning of the push with the poles, the hands should be positioned slightly in over the skis and not out at an angle from the body. Thus, the poles will rest at an angle, in over the skis, to allow for maximum backward push. Also the poles should be planted into the snow as closely as possible to the outside edges of the skis, minimizing the amount of energy wasted in pushing to the side. During the pole thrust the hands should follow a path as close to the body as possible, closing behind the thighs and almost touching each other with the wrist flick. Again, it is important to keep the pole thrust close to the line of travel, for any angle of poling away from the body or direction of motion tends to waste a component of the thrust in pushing the skier either off the track or off balance.

The One-Step Double Pole   Modifications of the double pole are the one-step and two-step double pole strides. In the one-step, the initial glide position of the basic double pole stride with the weight on both skis is assumed (review figure 3.8). From this position the ski poles are normally planted and the skier's weight transferred onto the poles for the subsequent push, but in the case of the one-step double pole the weight is transferred to one foot, either the left or the right. Instantaneously, the foot begins to press down and then kicks back with an extension similar to that of the basic diagonal stride. At the end of the kick, the poles are planted into the snow for a push to the rear. The subsequent arm push follows the same sequence of muscle activation and weight distribution as in the double pole stride described earlier. By the time the arms have pushed to a point adjacent to the thighs, the kicking foot should have returned to the initial glide position adjacent to the gliding foot. In completing the one-step double pole stride the arms follow through with the quick wrist action that brings the upper body forward and upright for the subsequent glide. For a further appreciation of the one-step double pole stride the reader is referred to figure 3.10 below.

The Two-Step Double Pole   For the two-step double pole exactly the same sequence of movements is used as in the one-step double pole stride, except that the ski poles are held slightly higher and are swung farther forward during the first kick (figure 3.11). This action allows time for a second kick by keeping the poles off the

Figure 3.10:   The One-Step Double Pole

snow for a longer period. On the completion of the second kick, the ski poles are planted in the snow and are weighted and thrust rearward to complete the stride.

The two-step double pole is normally used in situations where the track is too slow for an ordinary double pole stride and the skier wishes to increase his speed. Thus the leg work must be quick and powerful, throwing the weight forward onto the toes for the second kick and the subsequent pole action. By allowing the acceleration of the two-step double pole stride to bring him onto his toes, the skier can more effectively bring his body weight to bear down on the poles for a powerful rearward thrust.

Don't be distressed if you cannot fathom or execute the mechanics of the variations right away. The important thing is to develop a good, strong, and fluent diagonal stride first. The others will come naturally enough. If you intend to race someday, plan to do as much easy skiing as you can, because only after many kilometres will you finally get the feel of the technique and a sense of pace. In fact, some top racers eventually come to feel more comfortable on their skis than they do in street shoes during the endless kilometres of the winter months.

The technique discussed to this point is essentially the same type practised by all competent cross-country skiers everywhere. Certain small changes are sometimes introduced by individuals to accommodate their particular physical builds or capabilities—some skiers may accentuate slightly the reach of the arms during a double pole or change the limits of the rearward extension, but basically everyone practises the same technique. The minor modifications referred to here are merely stylish adaptations and need not greatly concern you as a beginner or weekend competitor. When beginning, try not to become too preoccupied with the quirks of style so that you miss the elementary points.

Techniques and Terrain: Application of Technique

The natural environment of skiing, the terrain, has so far been ignored in the discussion of technique. Hills and valleys, drifts and brush test the skier's awareness of himself and the techniques that he knows. Uphills, downhills, changes in the undergrowth require different movements and different expenditures of energy. The basic diagonal, while always a serviceable and comfortable stand-by, is not ideally suited to all conditions. You will want to adjust to changing trail conditions by using some of the variations mentioned in the last section, and, inevitably, you will want to employ some unique moves of your own to navigate the three most common types of terrain—flats, uphills, and downhills.

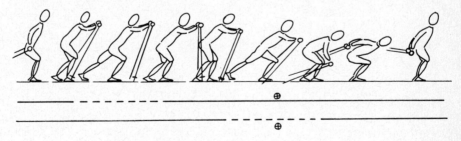

Figure 3.11:   The Two-Step Double Pole

On the Flat On flat terrain the diagonal stride is normally used with a hard, explosive kick and a full leg extension; the glide is as long as possible and there is a total weight shift from the kicking leg to the gliding leg. Although the kick-glide sequence looks slow and comfortable, remember, if you are in a hurry, don't be passive on the flat. The kick must be explosive and long to provide the greatest forward speed. There is a tendency to feel that the flat is the easiest terrain to ski. In fact racers often find that they begin to slow up here because of an unconscious drop in their kicking power.

The three- and four-step diagonal variations can also be used to advantage on the flat or where there is a slight downhill when the snow is fast. You can use the four-step to increase speed downslope in situations when the track is too fast for the simple diagonal and too slow for the double pole stride. Likewise, on long and very gentle inclines you can use the three- or four-step variations to break the monotony of a constant diagonal.

In wooded areas where the track is narrow or sinuous, the three-step can be useful on corners and in places where the track is partially obstructed by bushes or leaning trees. On corners the "outside" pole is pushed and the "inside" pole, whose motion would be short and awkward in any case, is rested. Moreover the extra push on the outside of the corner helps to make the skier turn. In a similar manner, the ski pole encountering brush or some other obstruction along the trail can be rested while the opposite pole works overtime.

If the flat terrain is rather bumpy, the double pole stride and its modifications can be effectively used on the downside of the bumps to increase the skier's speed. The one-step double pole stride can be used to advantage where a kick in the hollow of a bump is able to propel you up onto the

Figure 3.12: Techniques and Terrain

crest of the bump so that both poles can be planted and your weight and upper body strength brought into full use in the subsequent push. At the completion of the push with the arms, you will find your weight on the tails of the skis, an advantageous situation because it tends to shoot the skis forward. A word of caution here: this is also a very unstable position and is not recommended for downhill runs in choppy terrain.

Transitions from flat to uphill or downhill terrain offer additional situations where technical variations can be used to advantage (figure 3.12). The double pole stride and its variations are very efficient for making the change from flat to downhill terrain. Because it is a powerful, accelerating stride, the double pole is very tiring, and should be used only when it will produce the desired increase in forward speed. Thus, it should be used only in situations where the skis are about to glide

or are already gliding on downhills or fast flats, and where there is enough of a slope that the skis will slide easily. One example of the transition from a flat to a downhill would be where the skier approaches the crest of a downhill in a diagonal stride, moves both feet into the glide position, plants his poles just on the crest of the hill and starts a double pole stride. The powerful push carries him over the crest and down the slope.

If the skier approaches a downhill from a tight uphill stride, then a very economical, rhythmical way of changing from the uphill to the downhill terrain is to transfer from the "tight" diagonal (explained below) into a one- or two-step double pole making the final pole push just over the crest of the downhill. This variation throws the body weight forward for a good solid push with the poles, giving the added momentum necessary to start the wax sliding.

Approaching an uphill with residual forward momentum from a previous downhill can be an awkward situation—the skier must change his technique to climb the uphill, but must also maintain his forward momentum as long as he can before switching to uphill technique. The change to a tight, hill-climbing diagonal stride must be timed just right, so that the skier begins the diagonal immediately following the termination of the slide without ever coming to a complete stop. Providing that the uphill is not too steep, he can switch from the diagonal stride into a three-step diagonal and back for a mental and physical break while climbing the hill. If the speed is considerable from the previous hill, then a double pole is sometimes effective; that is, it can be used to extend the forward momentum as far as possible up the hill before changing into a tight diagonal uphill stride.

Uphill Technique   Uphills are a no-non-sense part of any ski trail, and they provide some of the most exasperating moments for the beginning skier. There are several approaches that you can take to climbing hills. In order of sophistication there are the side step, the traverse, the step-traverse, and the herringbone methods and, finally, the cross-country way, the "tight" diagonal. All of these uphill techniques, perhaps excluding the side step, are used consistently by competent skiers, and their choice of technique will be governed by snow conditions, their wax, and the steepness of the hill.

Side Step   For the beginner the side step is the surest possible uphill technique. The skis are placed across the fall line (the line of steepest gradient). Starting with the uphill ski, they are lifted and set down perpendicular to the fall line in a series of steps up the hill, surely a very slow and tedious method. You will soon want to progress to something faster. In addition, the cross-country harness is singularly unsuited to the side step, particularly in deep snow, because, when the ski is lifted, its tail tends to remain caught up in the snow.

Traversing   The traverse and the step-traverse methods are ways by which you can use the diagonal stride to climb the hill at an angle oblique to the fall line (see figure 3.13). By traversing the hillside you effectively reduce the steepness of your climb, and you can take as big a "bite" of the slope as your strength and the conditions allow. In addition, you need not lift the skis from the snow, but can slide them as you climb. Once at the end of your traverse, you must turn around to proceed back across the slope. This manoeuvre can be accomplished by taking your uphill ski and swinging it around on its tail so that you are facing up the hill with ski tips widely

Figure 3.13:   Traversing

spread and tails together. Next, transfer all the weight onto the ski you have just moved (this will become the new downhill ski) and swing the other ski around so that it now becomes the uphill ski, all the while supporting these movements with your arms and ski poles. Now you are in a position to traverse back across the slope to a slightly higher point.

The step-traverse is quite similar, except that the uphill ski is lifted off the snow and moved farther uphill with each step. The downhill ski follows the motion of the uphill ski. In either case the "bite" or the steepness of the traverse will depend on the gripping ability of the wax and how strong the skier's arms are.

Herringbone   The quickest, but not necessarily the easiest, way to climb hills is straight up the fall line, and the surest "straight up" method is the herringbone technique, illustrated in figure 3.14. This climbing technique is quite similar to the same practice in alpine skiing. The skis are placed together to form a "V" with the ski tips forty to sixty degrees apart, facing uphill, and the tails, as the closed end of the "V", pointing down the slope. By putting

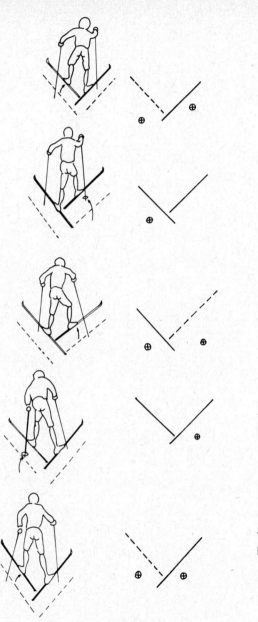

The left ski is moved forward, while both poles support the skier.

The right ski is set and the right pole is brought forward.

The right ski is moved forward, while both poles support the skier.

The left ski is set on edge and weighted as the left pole is moved forward.

The left ski is lifted, while the right ski and both poles hold the skier on the hill.

Figure 3.14: The Herringbone

all the weight on one ski and the opposite
pole and taking a step up the hill with the
other ski and pole, then transferring the
weight to this ski and stepping with the
other, the skier can effectively climb a relatively steep slope without slipping backwards. It is important to realize that the
weight is carried on the uphill or inside
edge of the weighted ski so that the force is
applied in a manner to make the edge
"bite" into the snow to give maximum trac-
tion. All the while, of course, the ski pole on
the same side as the lifted foot will be
planted and used for support, and in this
manner both sides of the body are being
supported and prevented from slipping
backwards. In reality, the herringbone is
very simply walking up a hill with your feet
turned sideways and your arms swinging
and pushing in rhythm, as if you were
marching.

   A useful variation of the herringbone
technique, somewhat faster, but requiring
greater use of the ski poles for support and,
thus, more arm strength, is to slide one ski
straight up the hill while the other ski is
placed at an angle to the fall line and is

used to support the body weight. You can
see that more strength will be required of
the left arm to support the skier having the
left ski straight up the hill and using only the
right as a brake to prevent backslip. This
move can be useful for skiers who have
made an error in waxing and find that they
have slippery skis but if possible it should
be avoided by racers because to do it
quickly demands much energy and
strength and as well it is slow climbing
because the skis must be lifted from the
snow.

The Tight Diagonal   The final way of negotiating an uphill is the true cross-country
way —straight up the fall line. Alpine skiers
are often amazed to see that a pair of skis
can be made to climb straight up a hill. If
you want to open a few eyes sometime,
jump between two bars on a T-bar lift
and ski up the hill in time with the bars.
People will whisper behind their hands, and
eventually someone will ask "What makes
those skis work?" Well, the answer is a

little wax, a little sweat, and a little technique.

When entering an uphill, a variation of the basic diagonal is used which is called a "tight" diagonal stride (figure 3.15). Similar to the basic diagonal stride discussed earlier, the tight diagonal differs in that the arms and legs are not fully extended rearward. The kick is not fully extended because past a certain degree of incline it becomes impossible to glide for any distance without losing forward momentum. Thus, the glide phase is reduced or absent.

Actually the length of the stride will shorten automatically when you enter an uphill. If you are in a hurry to get up the hill, your pace must quicken to compensate for the loss of distance caused by shorter strides. In order to quicken the pace and also to make the wax hold better, you must force your weight forward onto your toes. At the same time, you bend your knees (not your back!) deeply and "run" up the hill as if you were running up a staircase, shifting your weight emphatically from ski to ski but all the while sliding the skis forward on the snow. While the weight is moved rapidly

from ski to ski, the kick is terminated before the ski leaves the snow and the arm push is terminated at the hip with each stride. It is important that the knees are bent to a position above and forward of the toe, ready to spring ahead. The motion is quite like lunging up a hill on foot, but in skiing the ski is always left on the snow and slides forward. To lift the ski, boot, and harness with each step is just a blatant waste of energy.

When running a hill on skis, you must keep the body position of the diagonal stride. If the body is too upright, then the skis will make a slapping sound on the snow, and you will experience a loss of speed. If the body is too bent over, especially at the waist, then the skis will tend to slip back, even with good wax. Bending at the waist tends to put the skier's weight too far ahead of the middle of the ski, and the wax slips.

In tricky snow conditions the ski wax may not always provide sufficient purchase on the snow to allow the skier to climb straight up a hill. Occasionally the skis will slip, causing a momentary loss of balance and forward speed. One obvious answer to this dilemma is to stop and rewax, but this is not always possible or profitable. Instead, modified uphill technique can be used to advantage. If the wax works to some extent, then the skier can increase the climbing ability of his wax in two ways. By overextending the gliding foot forward and up the hill beyond the knee, the skier can lunge forward over the extended leg, thus ensuring that all of his weight falls on the ski to make it grip. This action, although not so efficient as the normal jogging motion, tends to put more weight onto the climbing ski and forces the snow crystals into the wax, making it grip better. If this method fails, then the skier should lift the skis off the snow with each step to allow the air to freeze the bottoms, thus providing them with the needed grip.

The side step

The herringbone

The tight diagonal

The step-traverse

Downhill Technique The idea of belting down a hill with such flimsy control—"a pair of slippers held onto a pair of toothpicks by the grace of the gods"—is probably initially the most terrifying aspect of cross-country skiing. Even seasoned alpine skiers seem to balk at the thought. But once you have mastered the balance of cross-country skis, you will find them quite manageable and stable. In fact, as your skill and experience increase, you will find that downhill running on cross-country equipment is an exciting and uniquely satisfying experience.

The single big difference between this and alpine skiing is that your weight must be transmitted to the ski through the ball of the foot. Because the boot is not held down at the back on the cross-country ski, you must apply your weight over the central part of the ski rather than on the tips as in alpine technique. Just the same, though, the knees must be bent and flexible to take up the shock of skiing over the bumps and hollows. Thus, the basic downhill stance consists of bent knees, a fairly straight back, arms extended slightly forward and outward from the body, and the skis weighted through the balls of the feet (figure 3.16).

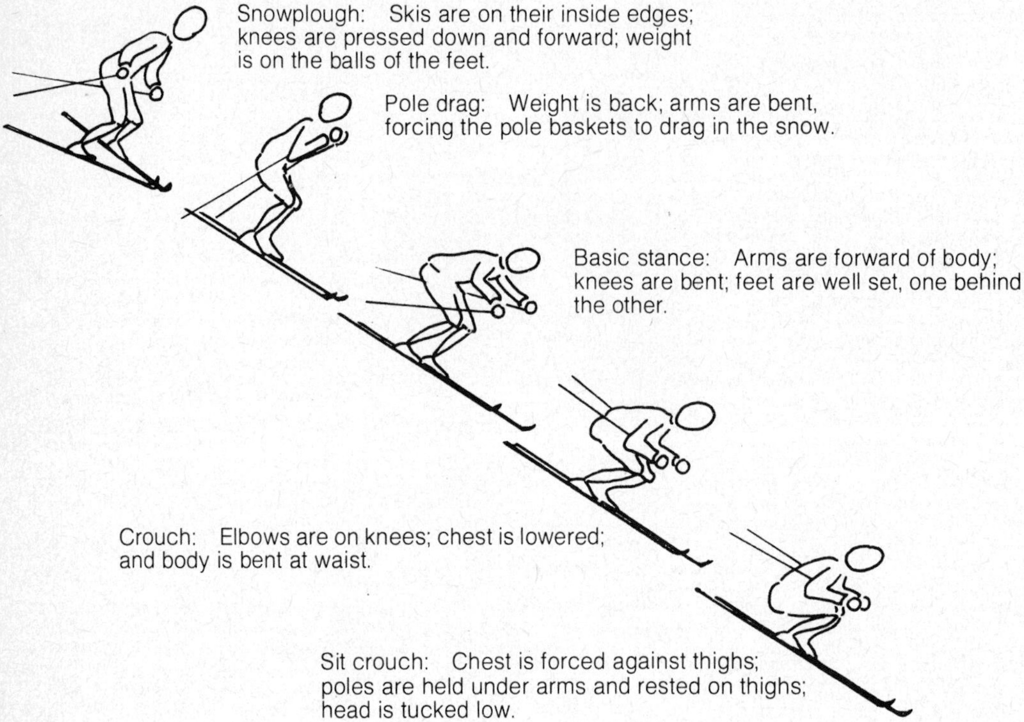

Snowplough: Skis are on their inside edges; knees are pressed down and forward; weight is on the balls of the feet.

Pole drag: Weight is back; arms are bent, forcing the pole baskets to drag in the snow.

Basic stance: Arms are forward of body; knees are bent; feet are well set, one behind the other.

Crouch: Elbows are on knees; chest is lowered; and body is bent at waist.

Sit crouch: Chest is forced against thighs; poles are held under arms and rested on thighs; head is tucked low.

Figure 3.16: Downhill Running

Slowing Down Invariably in the first few outings and while running down a hill you will reach a critical speed at which you begin saying to yourself, "I can't handle this. What do I do now?" Usually when this critical point arrives, you become frightened and stiffen. What to do? Well, obviously the logical thing to do is to try to slow your speed in a controlled and purposeful way.

Generally the speeds encountered on cross-country equipment are minimal unless you are racing, but if the need arises, downhill speed can be reduced in various ways. The quickest method to reduce speed is simply to sit down to one side. This method is cold and wet, but it is popular. A more elegant, if less immediate, method is the snowplough (pictured below).

The snowplough

The snowplough is virtually the reverse of the herringbone. The ski tails are opened at an angle of thirty to sixty degrees, while the tips remain closed and pointed downhill. With the knees deeply bent, the weight is pressed forward and out from the body through the balls of the feet to the skis. For more effective braking, the skis are raised on their inside edges and greater pressure is applied by pressing the knees down harder.

The snowplough is very tiring for the muscles just above the knees. While it is very stable, it is also inefficient, especially for the competitor who seeks a rest on the downhill. Where a more moderate degree of braking will do, one useful method is to place the ski poles under the arms, press them to the body with the elbows, lower the body, and drag the lower end of the poles on the ground (see the accompanying figure). Although hard on equipment, this method can be effective. Another favourite is simply to increase the wind resistance by standing erect or extending the arms laterally. By the time a skier is ready to practise this technique, he is already quite comfortable at the high speeds at which wind resistance makes a difference. In addition to reducing speed this method also provides a rest for tired muscles. Lastly, it will be evident to the beginner that the skier develops less speed in the first place if he skis away from the fall line.

Speeding Up If you are interested in a good, fast descent, you can assume a crouching stance of some sort in order to reduce wind resistance. The degree of crouch will necessarily depend on the roughness of the track down the hill. If the track is very good, with no steep piches or large bumps, you can almost sit on your skis by pressing the chest down against the thighs and knees. The poles are tucked un-

The simplest method of slowing down

In getting up, first place your skis across the hill

der the arms and pressed to the body by the elbows, in a horizontal position. In this manner you make yourself as small a package as possible. Your weight should be placed on the tails of the skis as much as possible during downhill running. The cross-country ski is quite similar in flexing quality to the alpine ski in that the tip portion is soft to absorb bumps; whereas, the tail portion is stiff and adds forward push when it emerges from hollows. Thus, by weighting the ski tails, you gain additional speed and reduce the friction along the length of the tips. Running hills in the above manner can be a lot of fun even for the experienced tourer, if the track is in good shape and clear of people and trees.

For rougher downhills, where there is a greater chance of the loss of balance and a fall, the crouch should not be so deep. The arms should be free and away from the body, while the feet should be set apart more than usual to provide better balance. When the chance of falling is remote, then the elbows can be rested on the knees and the poles held horizontally, resting between the elbows and thighs. Again the weight should be placed as far back on the skis as possible. The ski poles should never be allowed to drag on the snow while the racer is running a downhill, unless he is consciously trying to slow himself down.

Turns   The final aspect of skiing technique that must be discussed here is turning the skis. It is easy enough to ski on a straight track and run straight downhills, but few ski trails offer such constant conditions, and turning becomes a must.

The various turns required in cross-country skiing and touring are probably grouped best in terms of the speed of the skier during their execution. Slow-speed turns can be used on flat or gently sloping terrain, whereas, high-speed turns are used on downhills proper. Included in the slow-speed turns are the tip turn, the kick turn, and the skate turn. When greater forward speed is encountered, the telemark, the skid, or various alpine turns must be employed in order to change the direction of travel. Let us consider each of these in turn.

The Tip Turn   The tip turn is the slowest turn, used mainly on flat terrain to steer around obstructions on the track. Thus, when it is required, you will probably be employing the diagonal technique, and you can fit it very rhythmically into the basic diagonal stride by employing a slightly modified three-step variation. Study figure 3.17 to determine the sequence of moves that make up the tip turn.

From a basic diagonal the skier switches into the three-step, resting the left pole for a left turn (or the right pole for a right turn). Then, as he comes to turn, he flicks the right ski outward to the side by rotating the hip forwards so that its tip points across the path of the left ski tip; he then slides the right ski in front of the left, transfers his weight onto it, and removes the weight from the left ski. The heel of the left foot raises naturally, and at this time the left foot guides the left ski tip (still on the snow) forward and parallel to the right, the left pole is then planted into the snow and the diagonal stride is used once more. Actually this turn is a fairly complicated manoeuvre and usually comes only with experience and practice. A good exercise for this turn is to begin by running forward on your skis in a tight circle (with short, quick steps), at first lifting all of the ski from the snow except the tip until you get the knack of getting the outside ski to "tip around" the inside ski. Then slide the skis on the snow and try to obtain the same tip action. Soon you will be able to use the tip turn where necessary without even thinking about it.

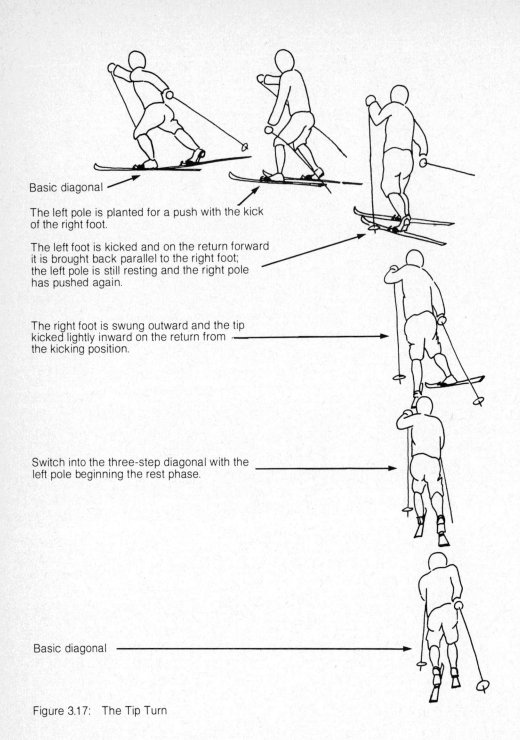

Basic diagonal

The left pole is planted for a push with the kick of the right foot.

The left foot is kicked and on the return forward it is brought back parallel to the right foot; the left pole is still resting and the right pole has pushed again.

The right foot is swung outward and the tip kicked lightly inward on the return from the kicking position.

Switch into the three-step diagonal with the left pole beginning the rest phase.

Basic diagonal

Figure 3.17:   The Tip Turn

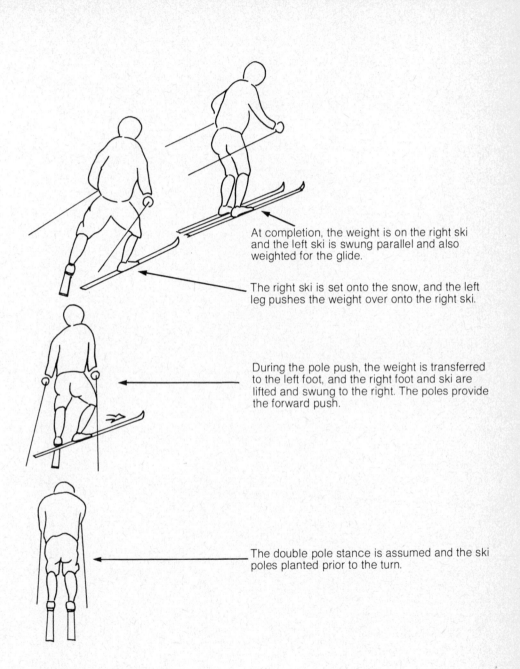

At completion, the weight is on the right ski and the left ski is swung parallel and also weighted for the glide.

The right ski is set onto the snow, and the left leg pushes the weight over onto the right ski.

During the pole push, the weight is transferred to the left foot, and the right foot and ski are lifted and swung to the right. The poles provide the forward push.

The double pole stance is assumed and the ski poles planted prior to the turn.

Figure 3.18: The Kick Turn

The kick turn

The Kick Turn   On gently sloping terrain the kick turn can often be used to advantage not only to round a corner, but at the same time to increase forward speed in the new direction (see figure 3.18). Unlike the tip turn, the kick turn uses the double pole stance. The ski poles are planted into the snow for the forward push of the double pole. While the poles are pushing, one leg lifts the ski from the snow while the other bends deeply at the knee, ready to spring up and around to accelerate the skier in the new direction. The lifted leg and ski are turned in the direction he wishes to proceed (i.e., left leg up to turn left and right leg up to turn right); they are placed onto the snow and weighted, as the other leg kicks off a ski well set into the snow on its inside edge; the ski is then brought parallel to the other. All of this takes place just as the poles have finished their push, and the combined effort of ski and pole tends to accelerate the skier in the new direction. As the acceleration wanes, the skier can either break smoothly into a diagonal stride or employ further double poling, depending on the requirements of the terrain.

The Skate Turn   At higher speeds (say up to ten miles an hour or so), the same sequence of movements can be used effectively to produce a series of "skate" turns. Although essentially similar to the kick turn, the skate turn does not involve the use of the arms to the same degree. During the skate turn the hands can be held about chest height and forward of the body, or, if the skier is in complete control, they can he held down by the thighs, supporting the poles out behind and up off the snow. The transfer of weight from the outside leg (i.e., the leg on the outside arc of the turn) to the inside leg is very rapid. In effect, you negotiate the turn in a skating-

like fashion by lifting the inside ski, placing it towards the new direction of travel, transferring all your weight to it, and then bringing the outside ski up and parallel quickly. Here it is ready to accept your weight for the next skate turn. Because the turn must be executed quickly, the kick off the outside is not so pronounced as it is in the kick turn.

All of the turns discussed are easily employed in slow-speed conditions on flat or gently sloping tracks or terrain, but once you get into big hills and find that you are approaching alpine speeds (ten miles an hour and up), then you will require more streamlined cornering, in which the skis remain on the snow and are not lifted as they were in the slow-speed turns. High-speed turns include the telemark (also useful in deep snow), the skid turn, and finally the alpine turns.

Keep in mind while studying these various turns that the terms "high-speed" and "low-speed" are used relative to velocities achieved on cross-country skis. Never would the cross-country skier attain the speeds reached by the top downhill racer or ski jumper. Nevertheless, it is possible to reach velocities of thirty to thirty-five miles an hour on large, open hills in an icy track. Considering the fragility and lightness of the equipment, such speeds are quite high.

The Telemark Turn   The telemark turn (see figure 3.19) is quite old, dating from pre-alpine skiing days when all skiing was done on rather long pine skis with a rubber-band toe harness, which left the heel free to be lifted from the ski. In this then-stylish turn the outside ski is placed out front supporting most of the weight while the uphill ski trails behind to act as a rudder. The turn is not very often used in skiing now, but can be useful in deep snow conditions where the trailing foot acts as a rudder to steer the forward ski around curves. In addition, if trouble is encountered during the turn, the skier can then put more of his weight back into the trailing ski. With his weight distributed over two widely spaced skis, the skier will have a better chance of maintaining his balance and preventing a fall. Try the telemark turn sometime in deep powder snow. It can be fun.

The Skid Turn   The skid turn lacks technical finesse, and as a result is easily performed and good for beginners. You simply force the tails of your skis to come about by twisting the lower body in one direction or the other. At the same time as you twist, you should also unweight your skis slightly. You can accomplish this by bending the knees more deeply than in the straight running position, thus lowering the body; then just as you are starting to twist your skis around, straighten up slightly. By unweighting the skis in this fashion you will allow the skis to skid around more easily beneath you into the new direction of travel. Of course, once the skis have come around, they must be edged to provide enough bite on the snow surface to stop the skier or change his direction; the degree of edging will determine the amount of skidding involved. It is possible to turn without skidding sideways by making careful use of the ski edges. But now we are getting into the realm of alpine ski turns, which is the next topic of discussion.

The whole process of the simple skid turn is not unlike coming to a stop on skates where the skater, by turning his blades perpendicular to his direction of travel and by raising them on edge, can change his direction of motion or stop. Probably when you encounter your first difficult situation such as excessive speed or a windfall on the track, the simple skid turn will be your saviour; and it will probably come to you as a reflex action.

Figure 3.19:   The Telemark Turn

Figure 3.20:   The Stem Christie Turn

The Alpine Turns   From the simple skid turn you can progress to the more complex alpine turns. One rather useful one is the stem christie turn. Although antique as far as alpine skiers are concerned, it is still taught as one of the steps to parallel turns and can be very useful to the cross-country skier in the bush and in deep snow. The stem christie begins with a snowplough position—remember, ski tails apart facing uphill with tips together in front. If you wish to turn left, say, then you will plant your left pole and weight the opposite ski (the right) by leaning your weight over it and forcing it to come around to the left to become the downhill ski. Then the uphill ski (the left in this example) is lifted and brought parallel to the downhill ski. Now you have changed your direction from straight down the hill to a traverse to the left; the longer you keep the downhill ski weighted, the farther you will turn, until eventually you will come perpendicular to the fall line (the steepest line) of the hill.

Needless to say there are many other alpine turns and all can be performed on cross-country skis under good, soft snow conditions. The one described above is probably the most useful to the cross-country skier, and hence the others will be left to your own research or skillful experimentation.

Technique Summary   In closing on technique keep in mind the following basics. The main item in a good technique is good balance, and balance is best when the knees are bent and flexed. As you have probably noticed, all of the technical manoeuvers mentioned thus far require a bent knee. On the flats and the uphills, the knee must be bent to provide the power in the kick; on the downhills the knee must be bent to cushion the shock of bumps and to lower the centre of gravity, thus improving balance. The back should be fairly straight and not too bent at the waist. Stiff, straight knees and a body bent forward at the waist are the first signs of an impending fall.

Another important aspect to keep in mind and to continually practice is the weight shift. Don't forget to shift your weight over from the kicking to the gliding ski during the diagonal stride especially on uphills. The weight shift is very important in that it improves wax performance in both gripping and sliding ability and allows for a stronger, more efficient kick. Without proper weight shift your technique might degenerate to an inefficient slapping of the skis along the trail.

Finally, don't be discouraged if you find some aspects of the technique presented in this chapter elusive. Cross-country skiing cannot be mastered in one or two outings. On the other hand, it does not require hours of concentrated effort in order to pay dividends to the skier. Be patient. First master the basics. Later you will find that the more complicated moves will develop by themselves during the course of your skiing.

CHAPTER 4

Ski
Waxing

The way in which you wax your skis may make or break your outing. Proper waxing is equally important in both touring and racing and for this reason an entire chapter has been devoted to this complex aspect of the sport. If the skis have been waxed properly, they should slide well in a forward direction and at the same time hold or grip on the snow during the kick. It is really the ski wax that provides the resistance against which the skier can kick and propel himself forward. Without a good wax job, the skis either slip backwards and forwards as if on roller bearings or, at the other extreme, they may "ice up" and stick to the snow like sandpaper to a cement sidewalk. No matter how experienced you become, there will be days when no wax seems to work and skiing becomes impossible. However, in North America the snow conditions are usually quite predictable, and waxing is a skill that can be learned. The toughest times are in the early winter, the spring, or during the January thaw when temperatures hover about the freezing point. For the enthusiast such conditions really offer a challenge and there is a certain pride to be had in "hitting the wax" on a difficult day.

The purpose of waxing skis is twofold. First, it provides a slippery, fast surface for sliding down hills and for the glide phase of the diagonal stride. Secondly, and equally as important, it provides a sticky surface for climbing hills and for the kick phase of the stride. A few years ago, tourists commonly used sealskins on the bottom of their skis, furry side down. The skin was fixed at heel and toe with the hairs facing the tail so that it prevented backslip and allowed sure forward glide. In recent times, the fish scale bottom and mohair strips have been used to serve much the same purpose.

These methods are extremely easy to use but unfortunately are limited in their effectiveness in the middle range of temperatures and snow conditions. With constant use, they wear quickly. While the plastic base slides well in all conditions, it does not hold on ice or crusty snow, while the sealskins, now not widely available in any case, hold but do not slide well. Ski wax is still the best substance by far to prepare skis to meet the snow.

Snow and Wax

Snow is composed of tiny, hexagonal (six sides or points) crystals which support the ski and the weight of the skier. Under this weight, the points of the crystals partially melt so that the ski really slides on an extremely thin film of water. The degree of melting will determine the slipperiness of the snow. Thus during cold weather the skis will slide poorly because the crystals will not melt so readily and their points tend to stick into the wax like small spikes. Conversely, in warmer temperatures crystals tend to melt easily and become rounded to provide a more slippery surface, and the skis slide well. Between these extremes snow has widely varying properties in terms of moisture content and crystallinity. Therefore, waxes having different properties to suit these various conditions must be used.

The way in which cross-country ski wax performs is rather interesting. When the ski is stationary during the weighting and kicking phases of the stride, the snow crystals stick into the wax very slightly and hold the ski to the snow. Then when the ski is slid forward for the next stride, the crystals are broken or pulled away and the proper wax will smooth itself into a slick, gliding surface.

Thus it is obvious that you must select the proper softness or hardness of wax to suit the strength and angularity of the snow crystals. In cold temperatures, snow crystals are usually more angular and pointed and fail to melt readily so that you will require a hard wax. If you do happen to try a soft wax in cold weather, you will find that the snow crystals will stick into the wax so far that they do not come out. Ice patches will form on your ski bottoms, and your skis will not slide at all. Thus it is important to match the hardness of wax to snow crystallinity.

Snow crystallinity also changes its character with time. Usually falling or newly fallen snow will have extremely angular and pointed crystals; after a few days the same snow crystals will lose their angularity and become more rounded, because the points have worn off, melted, or sublimated. Thus older snow will generally require a softer wax for grip and a good slide.

Needless to say you will not always have access to a microscope in order to assess the snow crystallinity; hence, you must use certain indicators of snow conditions such as temperature, age, and moisture content to ascertain the right combination of wax for the day. Each of these will be considered later in discussing the choice of wax.

Preparing the Ski

Ground Wax   First of all you will require some grundvalla (ground wax) to waterproof the ski sole of wooden skis. If you have purchased plastic- or fibreglass-bottomed skis, then you won't require grundvalla. Normally ground wax is prepared from pine tar and, if you can get it, pine tar is just as good. In years past pine tar was the trademark of the cross-country skier, and even the faintest whiff still reminds many an old-timer of the days of the crowded ski shack and the smoky barrel stove when ski waxing was really something to get the hands sticky and smelly. If you didn't spread the stuff with the palm of your hand, you just were not a real pro. Now the ground wax comes in tins with brushes, or even as aerosol sprays, and the application is easy and brief. Nevertheless, you can still spread the stuff with your hand, and in fact many good skiers still do so for best results.

Applying Ground Wax   Almost all new wooden skis come with a factory-applied protective lacquer on the sole to keep the skis dry during transit. This lacquer must be removed by scraping the ski sole with a straight edge of steel or glass and by polishing with steel wool before the application of ground wax. Such lacquers are not meant to replace ground wax and are poor wax holders and sliders.

In applying ground wax, it is important not to apply so much that the ski bottom is wet or tacky with wax. Apply and spread (with the heel of the palm) just enough so that the ski bottom has an even brown colour. Then take a small blow torch or propane torch with a flame spreader and heat the ski sole lightly and evenly up and down the ski so that the ground wax bubbles and steams. This action means that the ground wax is soaking into the pores of the wood opened up by the heat. Repeat the heating treatment several times; then take a clean cotton rag and wipe the ski bottom clean of excess ground wax by passing the flame over the ski sole with the right hand and following just behind the flame with the left hand and rag. Be sure that the rag is cotton or some material that will not leave small particles of lint on the ski bottom. Wipe the ski bottom until it feels dry to the touch and does not feel sticky. When you have wiped it sufficiently, the ski sole should be brown and have a slight smell of burned pine tar.

Clean the excess wax from the edges of the ski with the torch and rag in the same

Factory lacquers must be scraped off

Ground wax can be applied with a brush or hand

After heating with a torch, excess wax can be removed with a rag

manner. Any excess ground wax in liquid form on the ski edge or bottom will not hold the running wax and may freeze on contact with the snow, thus slowing down the slide. Thus it is important to wipe the ski dry and clean of excess ground wax to prevent snow from sticking to the ski bottoms, edges, or tops. To really make a smooth bottom, you can further polish it by rubbing it lightly with fine steel wool to remove excess wax and particles. Such practice is truly a must for racers, especially after applying fresh grundvalla before a race on a very cold day.

It is not necessary to apply this water-proofing agent before each day of skiing. It must definitely be applied to new skis before they ever touch the snow and should be applied at the beginning of each season thereafter. If you use your skis regularly, the ski bottoms may wear to a white, bleached wood in spots from time to time. Then you must rub a little ground wax over the wear spots, heat it, and wipe it.

A ski used in excessively wet conditions will require more attention to the care of the sole, and ground wax should be applied more often and in greater quantities. On the other hand, a ski used mostly in cold, dry snow will require less ground wax and should be wiped very dry so that it will slide well.

Care With The Torch   Blow torches develop a very hot flame. Even the smallest one can develop temperatures up to 2000°F and a very brief encounter between flame and ski can scorch the wood or ignite plastic. Burned wood soon wears away leaving pockmarks on the ski sole to ruin the sliding surface. Use of a flame-spreading device on the torch can reduce the concentration of heat, which is focused to a pointed, pencil-like envelope by conventional torchheads.

Remember also that wood reacts to heat by drawing away. Thus after excessive heating on its sole the ski may be arched considerably producing more than the usual amount of camber. To counteract this phenomenon you must heat the ski on its upper surface as well so that the ski will maintain its original shape and not be forced in only one direction.

Base Wax

The terms base wax and ground wax are frequently confused and used interchangeably. There is a difference in texture and purpose between the two wax types. Normally ground wax is made from pine tar or some tar-like substance which is black or dark brown; base wax is usually lighter in colour, often orange, and is a plastic-like, tough, and sometimes stretchy material. Ground wax is a liquid or very soft paste; whereas base wax is a solid tube wax.

Use of Base Wax   Base wax is used only in certain conditions where the running wax is likely to wear off quickly. In coarse, abrasive, granular snow, base wax acts as a binder to hold the running wax onto the ski bottom, whether it is plastic or wood. It is also useful as a binder to hold wax on in long races and tours or in rough conditions where the ski must slide over brush or conifer needles.

Notice, however, that base wax is used only in crusty or granular snows. In conditions of fresh powder, base wax should not be employed because it can prevent slide and slow the skis down especially if it "comes through" the running wax and makes contact with the snow. If you are certain that base wax will be required on the following day, it is wise to apply it to the ski sole the evening before and let it harden overnight. Curing the base wax in this manner will give you better slide than if the base wax is applied just before the skis are waxed.

Applying Base Wax   In order to apply the base wax you must have a dry, clean ski and a few pieces of extra equipment. A few base waxes will rub on the ski bottom easily and can be smoothed with a cork. Most base waxes are too tough to apply in this manner and heat must be used as well. Using a torch, heat the ski sole and draw the tin of base wax along the ski bottom in the wake of the flame, pressing the wax lightly on the warm ski sole. The whole operation is similar to cleaning the ski bottom except in this case the "rag" hand is holding and applying the wax. Now smooth the base wax by rubbing it with a cork in the wake of the flame. Any excess base wax should be heated and removed with a cotton cloth so that there is a smooth, shiny surface of base wax on the ski sole. Now you are ready for running wax.

Applying base wax

On the left, klister; on the right, hard wax

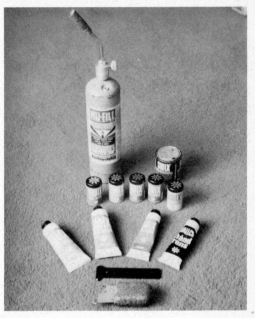

Basic wax kit for the beginner (one brand)

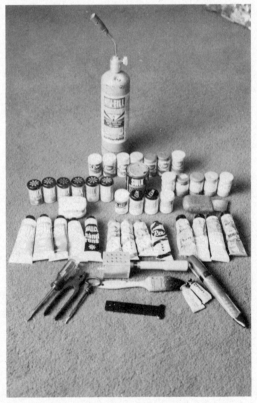

A more extensive wax kit for the serious skier

Running Wax

The running waxes consist of hard, soft, and klister waxes. The hard and soft waxes come in tubular tins the walls of which can be peeled back to expose the wax for rubbing onto the ski. Klisters come in tubes like toothpaste and have the consistency of treacle or corn syrup. The hardness of the wax is related to its colour and most brands adhere to a standard colour code. Green is the hardest and is used in the coldest conditions. The others are blue, violet, red, and yellow tins and blue, violet, and red klisters. For the beginner one set containing one of each colour is sufficient, although after some experience he will undoubtedly discover that certain brands of wax will perform better under certain conditions within their range. Different brands are discussed later.

Choosing The Running Wax Choosing the proper wax is not terribly difficult if you follow the basic ground rules in your first attempts. Later on, after many successful and not so successful attempts, experience will qualify the basic rules. You will come to recognize the conditions of track, snow, and weather in which certain wax combinations have worked before and you will not have to constantly refer to the waxing charts and rules. Nevertheless, the occasional review may be necessary if you are not skiing and waxing a great deal.

To match the proper wax to the prevailing snow conditions, you can refer to a basic waxing chart. You will see that to use the chart you must first learn to assess the condition of the snow on which you intend to ski. There is nothing quite so good as ski waxing to force you to become aware of the environment of snow and the vagaries of the weather.

In order to select the proper wax, you must first estimate or measure three characteristics of the snow—the type, the moisture content, and the temperature.

Waxing Examples

	Snow Temp.	Snow Type	Wax Chart Says	Comments
1.	5°F	New snow	Light green (100%)	Apply 2-3 thin layers smoothing each in turn.
2.	15°F	Old snow	Either green or blue (60% green, 40% blue)	Apply 2-3 heavy layers of green smoothing each, then add blue under the foot if more grip is needed.
3.	20°F	Old snow	Either green or blue. Chart says more blue: 15% green, 85% blue.	Apply one layer of green, smooth, then 2 layers of blue smoothing each.
4.	30°F	Old snow	Purple with red: 55% purple, 45% red.	Apply 2-3 layers of purple smoothing each, then add 1-2 layers of red under the foot.
5.	32°F	New snow	60% Purple 40% Yellow	Apply 2-3 layers of purple (heavy) smoothing each, then add a very thin layer of yellow under foot.
6.	27°F	Coarse, wet recrystallized snow	30% Blue Klister 70% Violet Klister	Apply a thin layer of blue klister over whole ski bottom, then add thin violet layer over it. Heat with torch and mix with brush or stick.
7.	35°F	Coarse, wet recrystallized snow with icy parts	40% Red Klister 60% Silver Klister	Apply thin layer of red to whole ski sole, then add silver to whole ski sole. Add more red over silver under the foot for more grip. Heat and mix with brush.
8.	10°F	Crusty, coarse snow with ice	100% Blue Klister	Apply thin layer of blue klister. Heat and spread with brush or stick. Freeze outside, add green hard wax blue klister, and smooth with cork.

Wax Chart

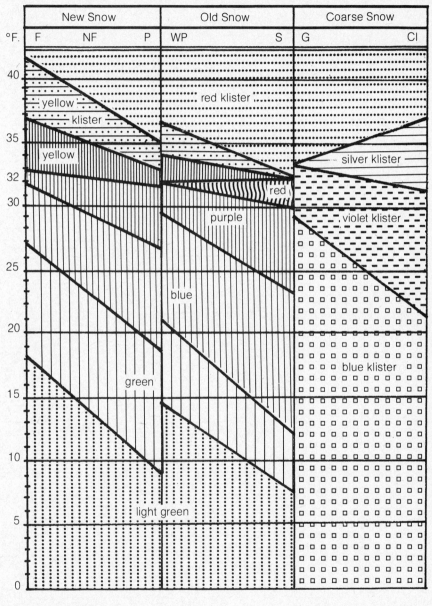

F = falling snow
NF = newly fallen snow
P = packed or coarse new snow
WP = well packed snow (several days old)

S = sugary snow
G = granular snow
Cl = coarse icy snow

Snow Type   Snow type refers to the relative age of the snow and thereby gives you an index of the angularity of the crystals. Falling snow is usually the most angular and crystalline. Hail, of course, is an exception and would be classed as granular.

New snow is that which has already fallen and is fresh and unbroken (i.e., not tracked or packed). New snow is generally considered as powder snow and is usually not more than a few days old. It has not undergone any large variations in temperature or thawing conditions and is quite crystalline.

Old snow has experienced radical temperature changes and will be changed considerably from its original texture. Warmer temperatures or the constant tread of skis will have broken down its crystallinity and produced a more granular snow.

The final class of snow is the crusty, icy, or very granular snow. Such snow is usually the product of several freeze-thaw cycles and is characterized by very granular or "sugary" snow or by a hard-packed crust, both of which are very abrasive on ski bottoms. Each of these snow types will demand differing ski waxes and differing methods of application.

Snow Moisture   The moisture content of the snow will be mainly determined by the temperature of the snow. The warmer the snow the more moisture it will hold and the more moisture the air within the snow will hold. Although falling snow may have a different moisture content than the snow already on the ground, and since you must ski on the snow falling in the track, it is best to judge its moisture content by the temperature.

A test of moisture content is done simply by gloving a handful of snow, squeezing it,

and then observing its character. If you can blow it away after squeezing it, then it is dry powder; if the snow stays pressed into a ball, then it is damp and moist; and if you are able to squeeze water from it, then the snow is definitely wet. Note that the snow should be squeezed in your glove and not in your bare hand where the heat of the hand can melt and hence compact it.

Snow Temperature   Snow temperature and not air temperature must be used to determine the wax. Often these two temperatures will differ by several degrees. Air temperatures can change rapidly, and often the snow lags behind so that on some days you may find that green wax will work even though the air temperature has warmed up beyond green's upper limit.

Snow temperatures give you a clue to the basic wax to use; the snow type and moisture condition tell you the upper and lower limits of its range. Thus, having measured the snow temperature and having estimated the snow type and its moisture content, you are ready to make the right choice of wax for the prevailing conditions. The waxing chart given in this chapter shows the various snow conditions and temperatures correlated with wax types.

Using The Wax Chart   It is easy to choose wax for cold temperatures but more difficult when temperatures hover about the freezing point. When temperatures really get warm, the choice again becomes simple and is limited to a single wax, red klister. Before studying the wax chart, keep in mind the basic facts mentioned earlier: the colder the snow, the harder the wax should be; the newer and drier the snow, the harder the wax should be. These rules offer guidance in borderline situations where the wax chart is not explicit.

Now we are ready to choose the wax for a hypothetical set of conditions. Let us say that the snow has been on the ground for a day or so, has been tracked by few skis, that the snow temperature is 18° F, and that the snow is dry (i.e., you can blow it away after squeezing it in a gloved hand). How can we use this information and the chart to determine the wax?

First use the snow temperature (18°F) to enter the chart; that is, find the temperature on the left side and then progress across the chart along the temperature line to the "new snow" column. You will find that green is the wax for these conditions.

If the snow was old or more granular but was still dry and still at 18° F, you would continue further across the chart, entering into the next snow type, old snow. Now you can see that there are two possible wax types, green and blue. In a situation such as this, you would choose the colder and thus harder wax first (green). Apply it, try it, and if the result is a slippery ski (i.e., if backslip results), then you must apply some blue wax over the green to improve the grip. Start by putting some blue under the mid section of the ski. If backslip still occurs, then cover the whole ski bottom with blue until the ski grips well.

As the snow gets coarser and the crystal points are worn down, the wax employed must also become softer in order to provide sufficient grip. Often the soft wax in such a case will not have to be applied to the whole ski sole; a small amount rubbed on under the middle of the ski may be sufficient for the necessary grip. In applying different wax types, one must always follow the basic rule of putting the harder wax on first and then adding the softer wax— except in a few special cases to be mentioned later. The reason for this is that when hard wax is applied over soft (if you can do it without first freezing the soft wax), the soft wax will wear easily and the hard wax will pull off of it.

Track Conditions and Wax   The geography of the ski track must also be considered when choosing the wax. If some uphills face the sun during the afternoons in late February or early March, then be prepared for soft spots of moist or wet snow in these areas. Often powder snow will cover shady parts of the trail even in spring conditions. Both of these conditions will require some mixing of waxes on the ski bottom. For example, red klister can be used for many days of spring skiing for wet snow, but if you find that sections of the track do have powdery snow or fresh dry snow, then you will have to harden up your red klister by melting in a little blue or violet klister. Soft wax can be added to hard wax best in the klisters through the use of heat to melt them together. Thus for some early spring conditions, klister wax jobs can come to look like the broadside of a rainbow when the skier tries to accommodate all trail conditions.

Applying the Running Wax   Once you have treated the soles of your skis with ground wax or base wax, you are ready to apply the running wax. Running wax should never be applied to the bare wood except for extremely dry and cold conditions, because it is porous and will allow moisture through into the wood.

Running wax must be applied to a clean, dry ski sole, and for convenience of spreading, it should also be a warm ski sole. Hard waxes are easy to apply in that they are simply rubbed on by pressing and rubbing to and fro along the ski bottom and subsequently spread either by the palm of the hand or by a more efficient "cork". Corks are not necessarily made from the material cork but now appear on the market fabricated from diverse types of styrofoam and synthetics. Their purpose is to spread the wax evenly and thinly over the ski sole.

Cross-country ski wax is best applied in

thin layers over the whole ski sole. The sequence is to rub on a layer, smooth it with a cork, apply another thin layer, cork, and repeat. The number of layers required will vary. If the trail or the race is long, 30 to 50 kilometres in length, then you must apply several layers (5 to 6 at least); you may even use base wax if the snow is exceptionally coarse-grained or granular. Thus the rougher the snow the more layers you must put on. If one or two layers of wax will not grip sufficiently, then you might add several more to improve the grip. The thicker the wax the better will be the grip. However, there will be a corresponding loss of slide. If the snow is cold and new, a few layers will do the job, but as the snow ages or dampens more layers or a softer wax type will be required.

The number of layers is particularly crucial at the freezing point. New snow at about 32° F requires a very thin layer of yellow over the whole ski. If the ski does not grip, put an additional, very thin layer under the middle (i.e., under the foot) of the ski. Usually this will suffice. If you have in your exuberence plastered on too much yellow and the ski will not slide, you can remove some with a scraper or rub some purple hard wax over the top. To do this, as described earlier, you must place the skis outside and freeze the yellow so that it hardens. The purple is applied outside and is corked into the yellow on the ski sole.

This type of waxing is really done by trial and error. The chart gives you a starter and from that you must decide whether to mix a softer or harder wax to obtain the best combination to fit borderline conditions. To do this you must have a sound grasp of the principles mentioned earlier and some experience to boot. Do not be afraid to try different combinations.

Wax should be applied over the whole ski sole, including the tips. Paraffin wax can be used on the tops of the skis to keep the

Applying the wax

Smoothing the wax with a cork

Smoothing the wax by hand

snow from clogging there on wet days. This practice is especially important for racers who already have enough weight to push around the track without an additional half pound of snow stuck on the top surface of the skis.

Wax and the Groove   Some authorities feel that the groove of the ski should not be waxed when using klister, but should be covered with a hard wax so that the ski retains its tracking characteristic. In deciding, however, you should consider that the groove constitutes about 20 per cent of the ski sole and that there may be a need to wax it with the running wax in order to get an effective grip. On the other hand, be careful not to completely fill the groove with klister for not only does it destroy the tracking quality of the ski, but it also produces an overly thick layer of wax which could ice up and present problems. The pressure of contact on the snow is least in the middle of the ski along the groove, and an excess of wax or too soft a wax here will ice quickly. With this in mind it is good policy to add soft waxes and klisters close to the edges first, to grip on damp snow. If the skis still will not grip, the soft wax is added to the whole ski bottom.

Various types of corks

The Wax Cork

The cork is the most universally accepted tool for smoothing wax, but there are other instruments and techniques that can be applied to specific situations.

Smoothing corks should be of solid, one-piece construction. Composite corks tend to leave small bits of material stuck in the wax, and although these are not so critical to wax jobs for cold weather, they will hasten icing of soft waxes in milder conditions. The small piece of cork or styrofoam will become a nucleus for the formation of ice crystals and prevent the skis from sliding well. Generally though, this type of thing is not so critical for the touring skier as it is for the racer, and many a ski has been waxed with the help of a cork from an emptied wine bottle. Any material that produces sufficient friction to warm the wax and spread it can be used.

Wax and Heat

On special occasions when the skier must wax for granular conditions and does not wish to employ base wax as a binder because the distance of travel will not be far, he can employ a torch and/or a waxing iron to heat and spread the wax. When heated, the wax impregnates itself into the wood of the ski sole and becomes a little more tenacious than usual so that it does not wear off immediately. If the wax is heated with an open flame and cooled, it will be somewhat more slippery than if it is applied cold; hence, it is always wise to apply at least one more cold layer over heated wax.

The Waxing Iron

Smoothing the wax with an iron offers the best way to obtain a very smooth, polished surface with little expenditure of elbow grease. For extremely cold conditions the iron (or a putty knife) can be used effectively to produce a smooth, slippery wax surface. Waxing irons are sold with small tablets which burn and provide the heat, but you may find it easier to heat the iron with a propane torch.

To use the iron, first apply a heavy layer of wax to the ski and then run the flat side of the hot iron along the ski sole beginning at the tail and moving to the tip of the ski. When the iron cools, reheat it and continue. Once smoothed by the iron, the wax can be polished with a solid cork outside in the cold air. The result is a highly polished, hard surface for gliding on very cold snow. The finer and colder the snow, the more smooth and hard should be your sliding surface.

When the snow is frosty, it has usually undergone some recrystallization or sublimation on its surface and the snow crystals are very pointy. In this case the wax surface can be left rough to reduce the contact with all of these newly formed spikes. One way of roughening the surface is to run the corner of a hot waxing iron along the length of the ski sole in a wavy fashion to produce a series of five, ski-length grooves in the wax. When the ski is slid onto the snow, the ridges between the grooves support most of the weight so that the effective ski sole surface is reduced. If the surface area is reduced, then fewer crystals can penetrate the wax and the increase in weight per unit area provides more melting of snow crystal points thus increasing the glide of the ski.

Applying Klister

Klister waxes are a nightmare for the beginner because of their sticky, glue-like character. Their problems can be overcome if you keep in mind a few basic steps in the use of klisters. First, klister wax must

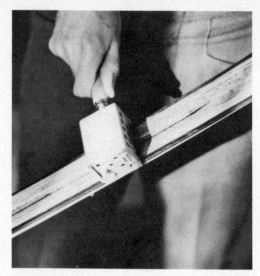

Smoothing the wax with a waxing iron

be warmed before application. Begin by squeezing the tube near its crimped end and work the pressure up to the open end (just like you would with toothpaste). Do not apply so much that the stuff is dripping over the ski edges or running down the sole. It is best to use a clean paintbrush and torch to smooth or mix the klister onto the ski sole. You should buy some hand cleaner or wax remover to get it off your hands and clothes.

The easiest way to apply klister is to squeeze the tube between thumb and forefinger so that you can apply a fairly constant pressure. Then, beginning at the ski tail, extrude a strip of the wax onto the ski sole on either side of the groove. If you plan to mix klisters, then extrude the various types you will need at this time along the sections of the ski. For example, for a peculiar set of spring conditions, you may want to have blue klister along the whole length with violet along the tips and tails interfingered with strips of red under the mid-section.

Once you have finished mixing or ex-

Apply klister in strips from ski tail to tip

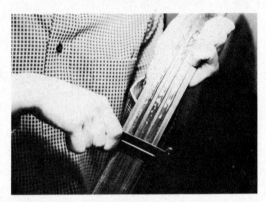

Klister can be spread with a stick by drawing it on edge from the ski's tail to its tip

Klister can be spread by using a torch and a brush from the ski's tail to its tip

truding, you can then heat the klister with a torch and begin spreading it with a paintbrush, always wielding the brush in a forward direction from the tail to the tip of the ski. This technique is the easiest for spreading klisters but there are others.

Some skiers prefer to spread the strips of wax by drawing a flat stick or plastic scraper (often provided with the klister) from the ski tail to the tip, spreading the wax out onto the ski sole. This technique allows the lateral variation of waxes across the ski sole without too much mixing. Such a method is useful if you must ski on a wet, icy track with many downhills and turns so that you will need to edge or brake a lot. You might apply strips of blue klister along the edges of the ski sole while using softer violet or red in the centre. The blue is harder and tougher than the others so that when the ski is edged, the blue protects the inner waxes and simultaneously provides a slippery surface for gliding on the edges. On the other hand, when the ski is placed flat on the wet snow, the softer inner waxes provide the grip.

Cooling and Wearing in Wax

The skis must stand for a while outside in the cold air after being waxed before they are put on the snow and used. The wax should be given time to come to the same temperature as the air and snow slowly. Otherwise condensation will occur and the skis will be slippery in moist snow or will freeze in cold snow. As well, the skis should be used for about one-half to one kilometre before a safe judgment on wax can be made. It takes this long for the wax to properly wear in and provide its best grip and glide.

There are many combinations and possible techniques for the choice and application of ski wax. The beginner need only be concerned with basic one-wax waxing until experience provides the insight necessary for more meticulous combinations. On the other hand, the racer or competitor will need to pay special attention to his waxing techniques and must make a keen effort to become most proficient with their use.

Grip or Slide?

To achieve good grip in waxing is easy. You simply keep adding more wax or a softer wax until the ski grips. To achieve a good slide concurrently is not always so easy. For the tourer a good grip is probably the more important because it makes hill climbing a lot easier. Conversely, the racer must stress good slide.

The topography of the trail will determine the preference for a good slide or a good grip. If the track is fairly flat with gentle uphills, the skier can choose a slippery wax job with maximum slide and marginal grip, relying on his arm strength to provide the necessary power to get up the small hills. Of course, with good glide the skis will slide well on the downhills and flats, an advantage over skis with better grip but poorer slide.

Thus the serious cross-country skier must come to know the amount of grip he requires and the amount of slide he needs to perform his best through experience.

Wax Removal

Once the tour or race is over and you have had a successful day, what must you do with the wax job? For touring or everyday skiing the wax need not be removed after each day's outing. If you expect the weather and ski conditions to be similar on the following day, then leave the same wax on and if necessary just add a little more to improve its performance. Some tourers get

through the whole season using only two wax types and just keep adding one or the other, never cleaning their skis. Needless to say, they must choose the days on which they go out to fit the wax on their skis, but in North America the pleasant weather in winter usually requires green or blue hard wax. This practice is fine with the use of cold waxes but is not such a good idea with soft waxes. Klisters particularly have an affinity for picking up conifer needles and other debris; they thus become dirty and lose their slide. Nevertheless, on relatively clean snow they can be reused for a day or two under similar conditions.

The racer must definitely clean his skis to remove wax before each race. Even hard wax will pick up enough dirt from the track and become sufficiently pitted to require a rewaxing. In the race seconds count, and the racer must use all of the advantages at his disposal.

Torching

If you find it necessary to remove the running wax from previous trips then there are several alternatives that can be employed. The universal tools for wax removal are the torch and rag. By heating the wax and wiping it from the ski sole in much the same manner as you did earlier with the ground wax, you can effectively clean the ski bottom. The bottom should be heated and wiped until dry when tested by your finger. If you leave a fingerprint, there is still wax on the ski, if not, then it is clean.

Scraping

By first scraping the ski sole with a plastic scraper (car window ice-scrapers are fine), you can make torching that much easier and shorter. Be sure to employ plastic or some material that does not scrape off the

Use a scraper to remove most of the wax

Heat and then wipe off the remaining wax with a rag

wood. The purpose here is to clean off the wax and not to plane down the ski. It is a good idea to put as little heat as possible onto your ski bottoms. Prolonged exposure to heat may char the wood or put undue stress on glued laminations, thus causing future separation. Removing most of the wax in a cold state by scraper reduces the amount of heating required, especially in the case of klisters.

Solvent

There are some wax solvents available which dissolve the wax on the ski sole. Care must be taken with the use of commercial cleaning fluids, however. Some have an oil base and will penetrate the wood bottom to prevent running wax from adhering to the ski sole later. Similarly, gasoline is not suitable because on evaporation it leaves behind residues of lead and other additives which will interfere with the next wax coat. If you must use gasoline, then use naptha or white gas which are non-leaded.

For removal of wax from plastic-bottomed skis where the chance of igniting the ski sole with the torch is high, non-leaded gasoline or varsol are good choices. The gasoline does not sink into the plastic and a light rub with fine steel wool will remove any residues or resistant wax. Even for wood-bottomed skis a rub-down with fine steel wool after the torch treatment will produce a very clean surface for the next wax application.

Different Brands

Different brands of waxes vary somewhat in their properties, and even though similar colours amongst brands represent wax for the same range of conditions, one brand may be better than another at the extremities of the range. For example, green Swix will work in snow of a higher temperature and moisture content than will say green Ex-elite, but basically they are for the same range of snow conditions. It is in the extremities of each range that knowledge of the variation in brands becomes important, especially for racers. They would find better slide from green Swix alone than from green Ex-elite which may need some blue under the middle of the ski to achieve good grip.

Some of these variations are mentioned below, but remember that there is no gospel on waxing. Different people might experience different results due to variations in their weight, strength, and skiing ability and due to unique local conditions of climate and snow.

There are many different brands of waxes, but the ones most commonly used in North America are Swix, Rex, Rode, and Ex-elite waxes made in Norway, Finland, Italy, and Sweden respectively. Thus the following discussion of brands has been limited only to these few.

Comparison of Brands   Note that all of the waxes mentioned here will work. Some are better than others for specific conditions.

Cold Specials

Rode:
(pale green)
— fastest all-around wax for colder temperatures.
— good in new snow and will work up to about 16° F in new snow.
— requires 1-2 km to produce best grip.

Rex:
(pale green)
— good in a more limited range than Rode.
— difficult to apply and best in older snow where it gives good grip and good slide.

Ex-elite:
(black)
— relatively soft.
— gives best performance in soft snow or frosty snow on a loose track.

Swix:
(pale green)
— toughest but slowest of all hard specials.
— slides relatively well in sugary, granular snow.
— often ironed on as a binder for Rode special in longer races.

Greens

Ex-elite:
(light green)
— fastest, all-around wax for temperatures in green range.
— gives good grip, but is prone to icing on damp snow especially if skis are not cooled before being placed onto snow.
— very good on packed trail.

Rode:
(dark green)
— relatively softer than Ex-elite.
— easily applied.
— works best in warmer end of green range and doesn't slide well at colder end.

Rex:
(green)
— hardest of greens.
— best at colder end of green range on hard-packed trails.

Swix:
(green)
— tough and slow but excellent for touring.
— works best at warmer end of its range.
— can be used as a binder for Ex-elite or Rode, but it must be used sparingly due to its poorer gliding quality.

Blues

Ex-elite:
(blue)
— fastest of the blue waxes, but tends to be slower in damp snow.
— grip is poor in damp conditions where snow polishes in track.
— especially good slide and grip at cold end of its range.

Rex:
(blue)
— works best at colder end of blue range.
— tends to be slippery on moist snow.

Rode:
(dark blue)
— slow in moist conditions.
— tends to produce suction.
— slowest of blues but easy to apply.

Swix:
(light blue)
— tough but somewhat slow.
— easily applied.
— best at the upper end of blue range and in granular snow.

Purples

Rex:
(violet)
—best for fairly damp snow in the range and good in combination with Rex yellow.
—very good grip in moisture laden snow which is rapidly cooling.
—toughest of purples thus good in granular conditions.

Swix:
(purple)
—best for drier, colder snow in the purple range.
—provides best slide in these conditions if applied as a thin layer mixed with blue.

Rode:
(violet)
—soft and best in mid range of purples.

Ex-elite:
(violet)
—best at cold end of purple range.

Reds

Rex:
(red)
—good in damp granular snow but slow in new snow.

Rode:
(red)
—best in granular snow.
—very tough wax.

Ex-elite:
(deep-red)
—best in granular, but very prone to icing in new snow or moderately old snow.

Swix:
(red)
—very soft and greasy wax.
—prone to icing and wears poorly in granular, probably best in new snow but seldom used.

Yellows

Rex:
(yellow)
—best grip.
—most used of the yellows.
—excellent in thin layer for new snow, but slide is poor when snow becomes wet.

Rode:
(pale yellow)
—next best yellow.
—less prone to icing than Rex.
—better at colder end of yellow range.

Swix:
(brownish (yellow)
—hardest of yellows.
—best at dry end of range but prone to freezing.

Ex-elite:
(pale yellow)
—difficult to find exact conditions for this brand.
—very prone to freezing.

Red Klisters

Rode:
(red)
—best red klister.
—reasonably hard and durable.
—performs well in a track with wet slushy snow and occasional icy snow.
—in sopping snow somewhat slow.
—slips slightly in new snow.

Rex:
(red)
—best grip.
—best in wet granular.
—tends to be slow and prone to icing in new snow.
—often used underfoot to improve grip of Rode above.

Swix:
(red)
—best for old, coarse, wet snow.

Swix:
(yellow)
—best for new, wet snow.

Ex-elite:
(pale yellow)
—for new snow.
—not much used.

Purple Klisters

Swix:
(violet)
—best of the purple klisters.
—works best when snow is icy and wet.
—freezes easily in dry snow and becomes very slow.

Rex:
(violet)
—works well in icy and granular snow at dry end of purple klister range.

Rode:
(violet)
—works best in moist granular snow.
—poor in wet conditions, develops suction and tends to be slow.

Blue Klisters

Swix:
(blue)
—fastest of the blues.
—works well in icy or granular, moist snow.
—slippery in wet conditions.

Rex:
(blue)
—toughest of blue klisters.
—often used as a binder for softer klisters.
—gives good grip in wet, icy conditions.
—best all-around but very difficult to apply!

Rode:
(blue)
—slowest of blue klisters.
—works best in dry crusty or granular snow.
—develops suction in wet conditions and is slow.

Ex-elite:　—tar-based wax.
(brown)　　—prone to freezing and chipping.
　　　　　　—best at upper range of blue klisters.

Silver Klisters
Rex:　　—best in icy wet snows.
　　　　　　—often used as a mixer to harden up
　　　　　　　softer klisters for wet abrasive
　　　　　　　snow.

Rode:　　—best at dryer end of silver range.
　　　　　　—slow in wet conditions.

Special Conditions and Favourite Wax Combinations

Over years of waxing cross-country skis you will come to know several rather special ski conditions in which bizarre wax combinations will work extremely well. One such combination works very well on hard-packed snow (not icy) at very low temperatures like -10° to -15° F. Ordinarily at such low temperatures one should use an extremely hard wax such as Swix special or an equivalent, but by chance it was discovered that Rex silver klister applied to the ski sole while it is warm in the ski shack, then cooled outside in the air until frozen and subsequently covered over by one or two light layers of Rode cold special, works extremely well. The klister freezes to a hard shiny surface on which the cold green is polished with a cork outside in the cold. The combination provides very fast skis. If the temperature should rise to 0° F or so before the race is finished, the klister tends to soften, break through the cold green and reduce the slide considerably. Even so the application of klister on cold days seems to raise eyebrows, and if nothing else it will certainly provide a potent psychological advantage.

Another sort of waxing paradox is the use of red hard wax in cold conditions. Red Swix has proved effective in coarse cold granular snow at temperatures below 0° F. As with the klister, however, wax and skis must be thoroughly cooled in the air before they are placed on the snow to ensure that ice crystals will not spoil the running surface when the warm skis hit the cold snow. Some crystals are melted and form tiny water droplets on the ski sole which refreeze immediately as the sole cools off; this produces tiny spikes to ruin the slide.

A skilled racer will almost always have a few favourite combinations on which he relies to a great extent. One with which this writer has found success has been the combination of Rex yellow and Rex purple. It is useful when the snow is still slightly dry but tends to polish in the track after a skier passes over and when the temperature is hovering close to 32° F. First put on a very thin coat of Rex yellow over the whole ski, smoothing with the hand to be sure that it is evenly spread over the ski sole. Then take the skis outside and cover the sole again with Rex purple and cork it onto the cold ski. Let the skis sit for a while in the air, then try them. If there is backslip, add a little more yellow to the middle of the ski sole but not to the ends. The greatest pressure on the ski sole exists just under your foot so you can afford to have a little extra soft yellow there to improve the grip without jeopardizing your slide. If you put too much on the tips and tails where the pressure is less, then the snow crystals will stick in but not break off or pull out. If the skis ice up, you will need to apply some more purple. Be sure to completely brush or scrape the snow off the ski sole before applying more wax. Yellow wax is particularly susceptible to icing and if you rub a snow-laden ski sole with a cork, the heat generated will melt the snow and mix the water into the wax. Once on the cold snow, the ski will ice up again.

Another favourite which can be mentioned here is the combination of Rode red klister and Rex silver klister. In older wet snow in freeze-thaw conditions Rode red klister is an excellent wax for grip. If you think that you may run into drier snow on the track, you add some Rex silver to tips and tails. Silver is harder and tougher than the red and hence produces a better slide but poorer grip than straight red. Thus silver mixed with red on the tips and tails, where the chance of icing is greater, combined with red in the middle produces an ideal ski for fast slide and good grip. In addition, the silver hardens the red so that it does not pick up so much dirt, a factor that is very important in preserving good slide over long, conifer-lined trails.

There are many more unique combinations of wax and the best way to discover the ones that work for your strength and technique is to wax your skis conscientiously for each outing. Use a little reason, keeping in mind the basic rules and keeping within the basic wax types for the conditions at hand. Add a little softer or harder wax to the basic type to try to improve the performance and do not forget that these additions can be applied selectively to any section of the ski sole. Soft waxes usually go under the foot; whereas, hard waxes go on the tips and tails. Try some combinations and keep a record for future reference.

Waxing Summary

When waxing
1. Take the snow temperature and assess the snow type before choosing your wax.
2. Wax a clean, dry ski.
3. Use a base wax only for rough, coarse snow.
4. Warm the ski sole and wax for easy application.
5. When in doubt apply the harder wax for a given temperature first, then add softer wax first to the middle and then to the whole ski bottom to get the desired grip.
6. Remember, the more wax on the ski, the better is the grip but the poorer is the slide.
7. Remember, always apply softer wax over harder wax unless the softer wax is frozen.
8. Cool the skis outside in the air before use.
9. Try the wax for a kilometre before passing judgment.
10. If wax slips, try more of the same wax before going to the next softer variety.

When cleaning skis
1. Scrape off old wax, then use torch and rag.
2. Clean ski edges and tops.
3. Use non-leaded gasoline and non-oily solvents.
4. Do not heat skis excessively.
5. Try to heat tops and bottoms equally.
6. Touch up ski bottoms with ground wax when needed.

CHAPTER 5

Ski Touring

Basically all cross-country skiing that does not involve the rigorous discipline of competition can be ascribed to ski touring.

A general introduction to touring was given in chapter one. This chapter will concentrate on some of the more specific aspects of ski touring.

Extra Gear and General Advice

On a short tour of one or two hours you will need only the basic ski equipment. If you expect a change in snow conditions, you will also need a couple of tins of wax, a cork, and a scraper. These are especially important in the spring when temperatures vary radically throughout the day. A good choice is to select one wax of warmer range and one of a colder range from the wax that you start on. This allows you to correct for rising or falling temperatures respectively.

To carry the waxing gear and other personal items such as sunglasses and camera, you might invest in a small "bumpack" which can be strapped around the waist allowing maximum freedom of the limbs for skiing.

For longer, all-day trips into rugged or unfamiliar country considerable extra gear carried in a small packsack should be considered essential. Aside from extra waxing equipment, the following items might be of use:

1. knife and/or hatchet;
2. wire, screw driver, pliers, friction tape;
3. plastic bags, extra socks, light jacket;
4. sugar cubes, chocolate, or other sweets;
5. matches;
6. map and compass.

If you plan to stop, make a fire, and cook, then you will require an axe and matches.

Ski touring has come to mean many things. It can be unorganized or organized. It can involve people as individuals or in groups. It can have a specific purpose and destination or it can be just a vagrant wandering.

Wire, screw driver, pliers, and friction tape can provide many makeshift equipment repairs deep in the bush and may save you from a long, hopeless walk in waist-deep snow. Plastic bags make excellent "rubber boots" when worn either inside or outside the ski boots as well as providing a dry seat on a snow-covered log. Extra socks can relieve wet, cold feet and can also double as mitts for cold hands. A light ski jacket will be well appreciated when you stop for lunch and cool off after skiing all morning. When you are not planning on a fire and lunch, take along some sweet candy or sugar cubes to nibble on. If you are out longer than anticipated, the extra energy may be useful to get home.

When entering unfamiliar country, take along a map and compass, particularly if you plan to ski off the trail. The chances of becoming lost on skis are remote because you automatically leave your own trail to follow back. Nevertheless, in heavy snowstorms and in areas with many trails where your tracks disappear amongst thousands of others, you may experience some doubtful moments during which the compass will be useful. A good rule of thumb is to always plan your return trip to leave at least as much time before darkness falls to get back as you took on your way out.

When crossing lakes and rivers in strange country, take care. Avoid skiing near the mouths of creeks or rivers. Even in mid winter these spots can be dangerous when the current eats away the ice beneath heavy snow cover and weakens the surface. As well, frozen lakes often have water on their surface forced up through tension or compression fractures by the weight of heavy snowfalls. In cold weather this water forms instant ice on the ski bottom when one unwittingly skis into it.

At the beginning of your outing, set a pace that will allow you to get back without

extreme fatigue. If you find that you are breathing extremely fast, almost to your limit, on the uphills at the start, then you are most likely going too fast. By trying to continue at a pace beyond your immediate capacity, you will likely run low on blood sugar if you must go any distance.

Packsack suitable for touring

"Bumpack" can be strapped around the waist

A day's touring includes lunch on the trail

A blood sugar deficit leaves a person extremely weak; the ramifications of this aspect of strenuous exercise are discussed in later chapters. For now, it is sufficient to say that the condition is not unhealthy unless prolonged, but can present potential danger in cold temperatures. Along with the lack of energy, one becomes very prone to the cold and with inadequate clothing, one can easily suffer frostbite. Thus, it is wise to try to avoid this state unless you are attempting to use the technique for over-storing sugar in the body, outlined later in chapter seven.

Where to Ski

As already mentioned, cross-country ski touring can be carried on anywhere there is snow. Public golf courses and parks, hydro and pipeline easements, trails and bush roads, and frozen lakes all offer unlimited miles of open local area for skiing. In farm country open fields and woodlots offer interesting variety, but be sure to respect fences and private property.

On a larger scale there are many areas that offer developed or managed cross-country ski facilities across North America.

Bush-whacking and creek crossing can be hard on equipment

In Canada cross-country skiing strongholds have developed in both eastern and western Quebec, central and northern Ontario, western Alberta, central and western British Columbia, and in the Yukon and Northwest Territories. Some of the commercial ski areas lying within these regions and offering cross-country facilities are listed at the end of this chapter. Additional information on these areas can be obtained in the "Ski Canada" booklet published by the Canadian Government Travel Bureau in Ottawa.

Two extremely well-developed and well-documented ski areas are those around Ottawa and Toronto. The Gatineau Park Trail system near Ottawa is probably one of the best in North America. Each trail is well cleared, clearly named, and labelled as to relative difficulty. Trail maps are available from the Ottawa Ski Club, the National Capital Commission, and various cross-country ski shops in the City of Ottawa. Five lodges are maintained throughout the trail system to provide shelter and warmth to skiers. Only one offers commercial fare, all of the others offer only firewood, water, and stoves. With such a development, it is small wonder that some sunny weekends in midwinter often see the passage of three to four thousand skiers over the trails.

Toronto is notable for its urban trail systems and organized cross-country ski areas within the city. Many thousands of pairs of cross-country skis are sold annually in the Toronto area and the tremendous pressure for skiing space has led to the development of urban parks and golf courses into cross-country skiing meccas. In addition many areas on the fringe of the city have also developed cross-country skiing facilities. A small, informative booklet by Iris Nowell called *Cross-Country Skiing in Toronto and Southern Ontario,* published

by Toronto Life Books, lists and describes in great detail the various ski areas in Toronto and region.

In the United States the cross-country skiing boom has also acquired great momentum and many alpine resorts as well as exclusive cross-country touring clubs are offering facilities. Interested persons can get information on cross-country skiing in their areas by writing either to the Ski Touring Council, c/o R. F. Mattesich, Troy, Vermont 05868, or the United States Ski Association, 1726 Champa Street, Denver, Colorado. An annual list of citizen and cross-country races can be obtained from Tom Kendall, Chairman of Nordic Skiing, Eastern Ski Association, Brattleboro, Vermont.

Taping a broken ski saves a long walk

Spring touring can be fun…

but may include a dip in a creek if one is not careful

How to Find Out About Cross-Country Skiing in Your Area

Good sources of information on where to ski and local organization are the local ski shops, ski clubs, tourist associations, and chambers of commerce. If you happen to see a race announcement, then attend the events and you will likely get the picture of what is happening locally and where to ski. The Canadian Ski Association in Canada and the U.S. Ski Association in the United States can also offer information and help on a regional basis. Some of the regional offices and personnel for Canada are given at the end of this chapter.

Organized Touring

Organized ski touring in North America has taken on the form of tour races modelled after the famed Vasaloppet in Sweden. Tour races are not hard and fast competitions per se. They are organized for the purpose of allowing people to ski from one place to another along a prepared track. The challenge for some is to see how many kilometres they can do, while for others it may be to do the course faster than they did the year before.

Most tour races are annual events with many skiers looking forward to them and actually preparing themselves by going on progressively longer outings up to the date of the tour. Generally there are classes based on age and sex, and for those who wish to race the course, there is an open competition. Two very good examples of Canadian touring races set up in this manner are the Muskoka Loppet and the Canadian Ski Marathon.

The Muskoka Loppet is held annually in early January near Huntsville over a 30-kilometre track from Hidden Valley to Port Sydney. The tourers and racers start en masse at 10:00 a.m. and 11:30 a.m.

Beware of areas prone to thin ice

Touring gear must include waterproofed matches

respectively and soon string out across the lake and into the bush. The race entry is open to anyone in a ski club affiliated with the Canadian, United States, and European Ski Associations as well as any F.I.S. member. The touring is open to anyone regardless of affiliation. From a modest beginning in 1970 with 94 entries, the event has grown to well over 300 entries in 1974. For information and entries, write to the Muskoka Winter Association, Box 1239, Huntsville, Ontario.

The Canadian Ski Marathon held each year in late February runs from Morin Heights to Cantley, Quebec. It is one of the longest organized tours in the world, being 100 miles in length. Racers cover 80 of the 100 miles in a two-day event while tourers can cover from 10 to 100 miles over the two days. Entries can be as individuals or as two-man, four-man, and mixed teams with each member running a portion of the distance. Entries are now limited to a total of 2000 persons. For entries and information write to Canadian Marathon Ski Tour, Mr. K. Bouchard, Chairman of the Organizing Committee, Box 1168, Station B, Ottawa, Ontario, K1P 5S8.

Touring Awards and Time Trials

The Canadian Ski Association has established a series of awards for adult and junior cross-country skiers and tourers. The purpose of the awards is to encourage the development of cross-country skiing and to raise the level of general fitness in Canada. One does not have to be a member of a ski club or any group in order to participate.

Awards are made for achievements in touring and proficiency in covering specified distances during time trials. Total miles logged during a season makes one eligible for touring badges, while completing designated race distances under

specified times makes one eligible for time-trial pins and plaques.

Touring Awards The skier fills out a control card, totalling his skiing mileage after each trip including races and at the end of the season sends in his card to the touring chairman of his zone or division. Depending on his mileage, he becomes eligible for bronze, silver, or gold badges (see table 5.1 below).

Table 5.1 Touring Distances and Badges

		Bronze	Silver	Gold	
Men 18 and over		100	150	200	miles
Men 35 and over		80	120	150	miles
Men 50 and over		60	80	125	miles
Ladies 18 and over		110	145	190	miles
Ladies 35 and over		80	110	135	miles
Ladies 50 and over		50	75	100	miles
Juniors age	7	20	30	40	miles
	8	25	35	50	miles
	9	30	45	60	miles
	10	35	50	70	miles
	11	40	60	80	miles
	12	50	70	90	miles
	13	60	80	100	miles
	14	70	95	120	miles
	15	80	110	140	miles
	16	90	125	160	miles
	17	100	135	175	miles

For additional information see the booklet *Tour Canada With Us* available from the Canadian Ski Association.

Time Trials Time-trial awards are open to both Adult and Junior classes. Each season several races are designated by the zone or division as being time-trial races. Interested persons need only apply stating their age, and if they are successful in completing the course under the time stipulated for their age class, they are given a certified control card. By sending the back page of this card and a small fee to their divisional office, they can receive the time-trial pin or badge. Each skier is allowed to acquire only one badge per year and is allowed only five attempts to achieve it. Classes and their respective times and distances are given below in tables 5.2 and 5.3.

Table 5.2   Time Trial Data (Adult)

	Bronze	Silver	Gold	
Men 10 km				
Class A ages 18-34	65	60	56	min.
B ages 35-49	70	65	61	min.
C ages 50+	100	90	70	min.
Women 5 km				
Class A ages 18-34	41	36	33	min.
B ages 35-49	45	42	40	min.
C ages 50+	55	50	45	min.

Table 5.3 Time Trial Data (Junior)

	Bronze		Silver		Gold	
	Boys	Girls	Boys	Girls	Boys	Girls
Distance 2.5 km						
Class age 7	32	40	30	37	28.5	35
8	30	37	28.5	35	27	32.5
9	28.5	35	27	32.5	25	30
10	27	32.5	25	30	22.5	27.5
11	25	30	22.5	27.5	20	25
12	22.5	27.5	20	25	18	22.5
13	20	25	17.5	22.5	16	20
Distance 5 km						
Class age 14	46	60	42	55	38	50
15	43	55	39	50	35	44
16	40	50	36	43	32	38
17	37	44	34	38	30	35

Times are in minutes.

Additional information can be obtained from you local zone or division office or from the Canadian Ski Association.

Ski Areas Offering Cross-Country Skiing

Quebec
Owl's Head, Mansonville
Glen Mountain, Knowlton
Mont Sutton, Sutton
Bromont, Bromont
Mont Orford, Magog
Mont Echo, Knowlton
Mont-Ste-Anne, Beaupré
Stoneham, Quebec City
Manoir St-Castin, Lac Beauport
Le Relais, Lac Beauport
Auberge Yvan Coutu, Ste-Marguerite
Belle Neige, Val Morin
Mont Garceau, St-Donat
La Reserve, St-Donat
Mont-Ste-Agathe, Ste-Agathe-des-Monts
Mont Plante, Val David
Mont Tremblant, Mont-Tremblant
Gray Rocks, St. Jovite
Mont Habitant, St-Sauveur-des-Monts
Mont St. Saveur, St-Sauveur-des-Monts
Mont Avila, Piedmont
Mont Gabriel, Mont-Gabriel
Chantecler, Ste-Adèle
Sun Valley, Ste-Adèle

National Capital Region
Camp Fortune, Chelsea
Mont Ste-Marie, Lac-Ste-Marie
Calabogie Peaks, Calabogie, Ontario

Central Ontario
Georgian Peaks, Thornbury
Blue Mountain, Collingwood
Talisman, Kimberly
Hidden Valley, Huntsville
Limberlost Lodge, Hunstville
Fonthill Ski Area, Fonthill
Bay Motor Inn Ski Village, Chatsworth
Beaver Valley, Kimberly
Tyrolean Village, Collingwood
Mountain View Ski Hills, Midland
Cedar Springs, Orangeville
Nottawasaga Inn, Alliston
Fern Resort, Orillia
Horseshoe Valley, Craighurst
Snow Valley, Barrie

Oktoberfest, Barrie
Killarney Mountain Lodge, Burwash
Camp Wanapitei, Sandy Inlet, Temagami
Timberline, Kearney
Echo Ridge, Huntsville
Britannia Hotel, Huntsville
Tally-Ho Winter Park, Huntsville
Cedar Grove Lodge, Huntsville
Curlew Ski Club, Huntsville
Pine Lodge, Port Sydney
Divine Lake Lodge, Port Sydney
Muskoka Village, Gravenhurst
Madawaska Kanu Camp, Purdy
Mt. Madawaska Ski Area, Bancroft
Buckhorn Wilderness Centre, Buckhorn
Bethany Ski Club, Bethany
Devil's Elbow Resort, Bethany
Caribou X-Country Club, Bethany

Northwestern Ontario
Mount Norway, Thunder Bay
Centennial Park, Thunder Bay

Searchmont Valley, Sault Ste. Marie
Hiawatha Park, Sault Ste. Marie

Alberta
Marmot Basin, Jasper
Mount Norquay, Banff
Sunshine Valley, Banff
Kananaskis Range, Banff

British Columbia
Whistler Mountain, Garibaldi Park
Hemlock Valley, Harrison Hot Springs
Mount Seymour, Vancouver
Red Mountain, Rossland
Apex-Alpine, Penticton
Bugaboos, Purcell Range via Banff
Gibson Pass, Manning Provincial Park via
   Vancouver
Kimberly Ski Area, Kimberly
Fairmont Hot Springs Resort, Fairmont Hot
   Springs
Tabor Mountain, Prince George

Regional Sources of Information on Cross-Country Skiing

A. Canadian Ski Association
   333 River Road
   Vanier City, Ontario K1L 8B9

Contact: Mr. J. Armstrong
         Nordic Manager

Zone or Division

Northwest Territories Zone
Box 1651, Inuvik, N.W.T.

Yukon Zone
Box 266
Watson Lake, Yukon

Western Division (B.C.)
1606 West Broadway
Vancouver 9, B.C.

Alberta Division
Rm. 412, 304-8th Ave., S.W.
Calgary, Alberta

Saskatchewan Division
1002 Henry Street
Moose Jaw, Saskatchewan

Contact

Mr. R. Hill
President

Mr. F. Langbakke
Cross Country Chairman

Mr. J. Pettersen
Cross-Country Chairman
      or
Mr. S. Bjorklund
Touring Chairman

Mr. H. Lines
Cross-Country Chairman

Mr. C. Bennett
Cross-Country Chairman

The beginning...

and the end of the Muskoka Loppet

Manitoba Division
686 Fisher Street
Winnipeg, Manitoba

Mr. D. Wellard
Director of Cross-Country Development

Lake Superior Division
Box 1085
Thunder Bay F, Ontario

Mr. L. Lahtinen
Cross-Country Chairman

Northern Ontario Zone
1353 Gemmell Street
Sudbury, Ontario

Mr. D. Rees
Cross-Country Chairman
or
Mr. E. Hazen
Business Manager
or
Mr. E. Maki
Touring Chairman

Southern Ontario Zone
4824 Yonge Street
Willowdale, Ontario

Mr. E. Vuorimaki
Cross-Country Chairman
or
Mr. G.E. Hoffman
Business Manager

National Capital Division (Ottawa)
53 Queen Street
Ottawa, Ontario

Mr. P. King
Cross-Country Chairman
or
Mr. M. DesBrisay
Business Manager

Upper Ottawa Valley Zone
192 Agnes Street
Pembroke, Ontario
or
7 Hoffman Street
Pettawawa, Ontario

Mr. S. Ransier
Program Director, Cross-Country Competitions
or
Mr. I. Theilman
Program Director, Cross-Country-Touring

Quebec Division
881, est de Maisonneuve
Montreal 132, Quebec

M.A. Robert
Directeur Technique-Nordique
or
M.B. Faure
Directeur, Ski de Fond

New Brunswick Division
R.R. #6
Island View, N.B.

Mr. N. Vikander
Cross-Country and Jumping Chairman

Atlantic Division
70 Glenwood Avenue
Dartmouth, Nova Scotia

Mr. Lynne Mason
Cross-Country and Technical Chairman

Newfoundland/Labrador Zone
Physical Education Division
Confederation College
St. John's, Newfoundland

Mr. G. Snow
Cross-Country Chairman

PART TWO

Cross-Country Competition

CHAPTER 6

Competition

finally the cross-country ski race itself. This transition seems to be a response to an intrinsic human need to meet and conquer a physical challenge, in this case not only the mastery of a highly technical sport but also the physical barriers of the ski track itself. In this modern age of rapid transit and mechanization cross-country skiing is one of the few really physical challenges left.

The Nature of the Competition

The cross-country ski competition is a simple pursuit-type of race where the competitors start at intervals and the time taken to cover the race course (the elapsed time) is recorded. The competitor with the shortest elapsed time is the winner. Essentially the competition pits the skier against the clock; the presence of other athletes on the track provides only secondary motivations or goals as the skier tries to catch and pass those skiers starting ahead of him.

In longer touring, marathon, and relay races, mass or gang starts are generally the rule. In this case all competitors begin at once and the first one to finish is the obvious winner. Such starts produce a different aura to the race in that the competition becomes more of a man-to-man battle and the clock assumes secondary importance.

The relay race is a special type of event involving a team of skiers. It is the only cross-country ski competition requiring group effort. Usually the team consists of three or four skiers who must individually complete the distance, usually 5 or 10 kilometres. Each team contributes a skier to a gang start for the first lap after which the other skiers on the team depart as their man comes in from his lap to "tag" them. Skier one begins, completes his 10 kilometres, and tags skier two who completes the same 10 kilometres and tags skier three who finishes the race by completing the

The transition from touring to racing is natural but certainly not easy. For most people the desire to race begins with attempts to master more difficult and longer tracks leading eventually to the touring race and final 10-kilometre loop. The total elapsed time of the three skiers is the team's time for the 30 kilometres, and teams place in order of their finish. Although the team is the unit of the race, plainly the efforts of the team are really on an individual basis. Each member while on the track must perform as an individual and thus he must face up to the same measure of mental discipline and drive required of an individual pursuit race.

The Distances

Cross-country ski competitions all have one common characteristic: they are endurance events. The shortest Olympic event is 5 kilometres (3.1 miles) and the longest is 50 kilometres (32 miles). See table 6.1. However, there are longer events such as the Canadian Ski Marathon from Morin Heights, Quebec (north of Montreal), to Cantley, Quebec (north of Ottawa), which features 100 miles for tour racers and 80 miles for class competitors broken into two days (50 or 40 miles per day respectively). One of the longest single-day events is the famous Vasaloppet in Sweden from Salem to Mora, a distance of 85 kilometres (52 miles) over which the record time is around 4 hours and 45 minutes.

Times

Times over the standard distances vary from track to track but international 15-kilometre races such as the men's special 15-kilometre at the 1974 World Championships can be skied in as little as 41 minutes. The 50-kilometre race has been skied in 2 hours and 19 minutes. These times are extremely fast, representing an average pace of 13 to 14 miles per hour. The world's elite skiers are in such good condition that they can ski for 50 kilometres (32 miles) at nearly the same pace as they do over 15 kilometres (9.2 miles).

One of the remarkable aspects of cross-country ski racing is the minuscule time margins by which races are often won. One would think that over such distances the elapsed times would show considerable variation and that the winning margins would be large. But, in fact, even after 50 kilometres, the first and second racers may be separated by only seconds—even though they may not have seen each other at all. In the 15-kilometre race of the 1974 World Championships in Falun, Sweden, only nine tenths of a second separated first and second, and six tenths separated second and third. The fourth-place finisher was out of the running, finishing a mere eight seconds behind first. Such small time differences point up the necessity for clear thinking and an aggressive mental outlook which takes maximum advantage of technique, waxing, and terrain over every metre of a long race. For a mere eight tenths of a second could have been lost through an improper turn, a misplaced step, a backslip, a slight fall, a dragged hand or many tens of other possibilities.

Elapsed times for the various distances will vary from track to track and with snow conditions. In this respect there are no real record times except for individual race tracks and it is difficult to compare times around the world. Even times for the first lap and the fourth lap of a relay are not readily comparable because of the change in snow conditions on the track over the period of the race due to the passage of many skis or change in temperature. Quite often, one will encounter different types of snow from one location to another. The local geography and climate will condition whether the snow is finely crystalline, icy, or granular; it will also determine water content. Thus a comparison of times of

The relay race combines individual efforts

Table 6.1 Race Times

Class	World Championships Falun 1974			Canadian National Championships Quebec City 1974		
	Winner	10th	Best North American	Winner	10th	Slowest
MEN						
15 km	0:41:39	0:42:35	0:43:38	0:54:44	0:59:24	1:20:31
30 km	1:33:41	1:36:01	1:43:05	1:47:16	1:58:45	2:36:32
50 km	2:19:45	2:24:44	2:31:18	—	—	—
WOMEN						
5 km	0:15:17	0:15:57	0:16:12	0:20:26	0:23:58	0:34:39
10 km	0:31:25	0:32:46	0:32:46	0:38:52	0:48:53	1:04:51

Times are in hours, minutes, and seconds.

races on the dry snow of continental North America and those on the moister snow of Europe is at best inaccurate even without taking into account possible differences in track profiles. A skier's times will generally be slower in North America because the dry, cold, crystalline snow does not allow the ski to glide well. Sample elapsed times for the various distances are given in table 6.1.

The Requirements

Needless to say there is much more to cross-country ski racing than pushing and sliding a pair of skis over the snow in record time. The transition from tyro to master takes a considerable amount of study and practice consuming the better part of ten years or more. In fact, a technically competent skier with ten years' experience and moderate training is at a point in his skiing career when he can just begin to seriously develop his talents to contest the world's best. From this point he may take another five years to reach his peak. The person who wants to achieve excellence in the sport of cross-country competition must be prepared to develop slowly, devoting his energies to the mastery of the techniques of skiing and waxing; to training and building his body endurance and strength; and finally to cultivating a positive, aggressive, and disciplined mental outlook.

Technique is an important part of any sport, requiring hard work over long periods of time. Cross-country ski racing is no exception; the long distances involved require the crossing of rugged terrain with an expenditure of huge amounts of energy. Through the mastery of technique one strives to minimize wasted movements and to maximize forward motion and speed.

Over such long distances small technical errors can bring about premature exhaustion or the loss of valuable seconds. In his younger years the skier should concentrate on mastering technical maneuvers and de-emphasize speed and conditioning; it is very difficult to change bad habits of technique acquired in youth if they are practised into the prime skiing years when the muscles and mind become set.

Fast skiing makes tremendous demands on the whole body, especially on the cardio-vascular system (heart-lungs-circulation). The skier must be conditioned for such hard work. An excellent technique alone will not carry a skier to victory; he must also be in very good condition. If a weak skier loses as little as 3 centimetres per kick and glide of his ski, then over 1000 steps or strides he will be already 30 metres behind his better-trained adversaries.

Cross-country ski racing requires strength, agility, and endurance in different amounts for different tracks. In the faster tracks and shorter races, agility contributes to gained time on corners and starts; in long, 50-kilometre marathons endurance becomes more important in sustaining a physically demanding pace for two and a half to three hours. One should not be fooled though for all race tracks are demanding regardless of their profiles; even if the course is flat and "easy" one must increase his normal tempo to keep up with the winners. Regardless of terrain, endurance is the key. Unlike track competitors, skiers do not normally specialize in any particular event; hence they prepare themselves for all events by the use of a well-integrated training program of endurance, speed, and strength.

A large part of the performance of any athlete in a competition of long duration depends on his mental outlook as well as

his technique and conditioning. A large amount of mental stress has been removed from the cross-country ski racer in that injury is seldom sustained in the sport. However the long, lonely hours of training and the mental discipline required to push oneself for hours in a fatigued state do supply mental stresses. Through a well-planned training program and a system of short-term goals, the skier must build the proper frame of mind to maintain a strong pace over 10 to 30 miles, working each part of the track for maximum benefit. The application of technique to terrain requires relentless concentration where a mistake may cost valuable seconds but can be avoided by thinking ahead. Thus the requirements to become a top skier are demanding of both mind and body, and racers take a certain pride in the fact that their sport is one of the toughest with respect to physiological standards.

On the whole, those who engage in cross-country ski racing are self-motivated individuals. Many attempts have been made to coerce talented youngsters to train and compete without much success. The desire to train and compete must come from within; it cannot be "pasted" onto an individual. The best racers begin young and learn to enjoy skiing before arduous training is necessary to bring performance to top standards.

Cross-country ski racing is not a team event, and the skier's reward or reinforcement can only be achieved through his own efforts. The rules of the game are quite simple—you reap exactly what you sow. If one has been truant at his training, then no amount of desire or mental pushing is going to allow him to win a physically demanding race. The competitor must develop a sense of self discipline. He must train even when he feels like doing something else. Aspects of health and fatigue must be taken into consideration in a

Racing is for everyone

training program, but to really succeed at cross-country ski racing one must be prepared to work long and hard for eight to twelve months of the year. It takes many months to build up a good racing condition, but it takes only a few weeks to lose it.

Why Race?

Competition for its own sake is a good thing. It allows a person to develop a sense of purpose, to recognize and reach his own physical limits, to seek excellence. It involves travel to different localities which is an educational experience particularly attractive to younger skiers. One is able to establish friendships and acquaintances on a national or international basis; even though competitors are essentially competing against each other, there is still a sense of community.

Some History

Ski racing is by no means as old as the ski. It had its popular beginnings in the late 1800s and early 1900s in Fenno-scandia. Originally, ski racing was conducted on frozen lakes where the long skis and poles were easily manipulated. Norway began the modern era of ski racing and instituted one of the first annual international competitions in the "Hollmenkollen" races near Oslo each spring. Other major annuals came into being; the "Lahti Ski Games" are held in Lahti, Finland, and the "Svenskaskid-spelen" in Falun, Sweden. Winners of these major races are given as much recognition as Olympic champions; in fact, the races have taken on the character of mini-Olympics.

When racing moved from the frozen lakes to the bush, equipment changed and became compact and light as it is today. As well, racers discovered that a little training over and above the exercise from their work in forest or field helped them to climb the hills encountered in the new tracks.

The truly modern era of cross-country ski racing began with Nils Karlsson, Sweden's most famous ski racer. In the late 1940s and early 1950s he won virtually every competition, including the famed Vasaloppet nine times. Through his training habits and race efforts he became a legend in his time and received the nickname "Mora Nisse".

The decade from the mid 1950s to the mid 1960s, the age of the old men, saw the dominance of older skiers on the international circuit. Sixten Jernberg (Sweden), Veikko Hakulinen (Finland), Ero Mantyranta (Finland), Assar Roenland (Sweden), and Harold Groeningen (Norway) topped the result lists almost without fail. These skiers ushered in the age of intensive, long-distance training.

The mid 1960s, the age of Norway, produced strong Norwegian teams which

won virtually everything at the 1966 Oslo World Championships and at the 1968 Grenoble Olympics. Younger skiers took the cue from the older skiers and began to train intensively at younger ages. They soon took over at the top of the elite. Especially successful were Gjermund

Eggen, the hero of the Oslo World Championships, Paul Tyldum, and Odd Martinsen, all of Norway. The age of the youngsters saw skiers like Ivar Formo and Odvar Braa, both of Norway, contesting the world's elite in their very first year of senior competition.

In this era the rise of middle European and Communist countries is of significance. With the capture of a gold in the 1968 Olympic 30 kilometres by Franco Nones of Italy, these countries have become serious threats to Scandinavian supremacy in Nordic skiing. This is further supported by

The rewards: medals and recognition

the results of the 1974 Falun World Championships when Gerhart Grimmer (East Germany) and Galina Kulakova (Russia) were the best over-all male and female skiers respectively.

In North America cross-country ski racing has evolved in a similar pattern except that we are about ten to fifteen years behind and are trying desperately to catch up. Skiers in their early twenties are now, on the whole, the best skiers in North America; just four to five years ago the best skiers were invariably over twenty-five years of age.

These young skiers are the first products of an intensified training regime begun about 1965 when North America "discovered" the amount, duration, and intensity of training done by the best European and Scandinavian ski racers. Up until the mid 1960s training for cross-country ski racing consisted of three one-hour sessions per week with a race on the weekend. A few strongly motivated individuals spent time in Scandinavia at their own expense and knew what training was about. But for the most part North American skiers had an unwittingly casual attitude to training. Now one must train three to four hours per day, six to seven days per week, year round just to do well in the National Championships!

Over the past few years cross-country ski racing in North America has made a tremendous assault on the seemingly impossible time gap to the winner's circle. Now we are within 2 minutes of the best for 15 kilometres, 7 minutes for 30 kilometres, and 11 minutes for 50 kilometres on the average in the men's events. In the women's events we are even closer, and the possibility of a medal in the next Olympics looms large.

CHAPTER 7

Physiology of Skiing

these demands through a training program. In order to train in a sensible and healthy way, the skier must understand how the body functions under the stress of the hard work imposed during competition. He must come to know his physical capabilities, such as how far and how fast he can ski before he becomes so fatigued that his skiing technique breaks down. He must have a knowledge of physiology (how the body systems function) so that he can adjust his tempo and exertion during the race to allow for recovery or to maximize his speed. He must become a thinking competitor. Hence, the purpose of this chapter is to introduce the serious competitor and the interested tourist to some physiological aspects of cross-country skiing.

Energy and Oxygen

Energy can be produced in the muscles in two ways, aerobically (with oxygen) and anaerobically (without oxygen). If there is sufficient oxygen getting to the muscle cells, then the glycogen (glucose) in the muscle combines with the oxygen and other compounds to produce a high energy phosphate compound, carbon dioxide and water. On the other hand, if insufficient oxygen reaches the muscle cells then energy is produced without oxygen when glycogen combines with a phosphate compound and phosphorus to produce a high-energy phosphate compound and a lactate compound which eventually becomes lactic acid. Thus, basically the body performs by means of two "engines"—the aerobic and the anaerobic engines.

Cross-country skiing and racing is very physically demanding. In trying to cover specific distances over rough terrain in the shortest time possible great demand is put on the skier's physical strength, endurance, skill, technique, and motivation. Obviously, the skier must prepare himself to meet

The Aerobic Engine

Consider a skier skiing on a level track. He is quite relaxed, breathing moderately hard

Testing skiers in the track

but not uncomfortably. Most likely he is using his aerobic engine to carry on the work of skiing at that specific speed.

He is producing and expending energy at a rate that is compatable with the ability of his oxygen-transport system to supply oxygen to the muscles. This is usually called his oxygen uptake. Energy is produced and the waste carbon dioxide is easily "washed" out of the muscles to be carried by the blood to the lungs and expired. If he increases his speed, energy must be expended at a greater rate and thus more oxygen is required in the muscles and his oxygen uptake increases. At some point the skiers lungs, heart, and blood become unable to supply the necessary oxygen, and at this point the skier has reached his maximum oxygen uptake or maximal aerobic power.

The Anaerobic Engine

At this point if the skier continues to increase his speed, all of the oxygen in the muscles is depleted and the anaerobic engine cuts in to help out in the production of energy—but at great expense! The skier begins to breathe uncomfortably fast, but his oxygen transport system still cannot carry enough oxygen to the muscles, and lactic acid begins to build up. Extreme anaerobic work such as skiing at high speed up hills can only last a few minutes until the build-up of lactic acid inhibits muscle function. The muscles become still and fail to respond to the skier's desire to push on. The result is that he is forced to slow down the pace to a point where the body can again perform aerobically.

Oxygen Debt. By using the anaerobic engine the skier has incurred an oxygen debt in the muscles. That is, he has forced the muscles to use all of the oxygen store normally held in the myoglobin and also reduced the oxygen concentration of the blood. When the skier slows down or reaches the top of the hill and slides down the other side, he enters a recovery period in which the body begins to repay the oxygen debt and remove the excess lactic acid by oxidizing it in the liver back to glucose.

The physical condition and the maximum oxygen uptake of the skier will govern how long it takes to recover and repay the debts incurred by use of the anaerobic engine. Also the training the skier has done and his motivation will determine his ability to withstand the effects of a build-up of lactic acid. The rare, superbly conditioned athlete can keep it up for thirty minutes, but under severe exercise most people last only for a few minutes. Often this debt is not fully repaid during the competition, especially in short, fast, or long tough races, and it must be repaid during the resting hours after the race. Post-race light exercise at an aerobic level helps in recovery by expediting the removal of lactic acid and the replenishing of oxygen stores in the blood and muscles.

In addition to the above, the anaerobic engine is also inefficient in the use of energy-giving glycogen. The aerobic engine produces about twenty times more energy than the anaerobic one per given unit of glycogen.

Second Wind and Warm-Up

In fast starts, when the skier puts a sudden demand on the oxygen transport system, he may develop a pain or "stitch" in the side which disappears as the race progresses. This pain is a result of the lack of oxygen in the diaphragm which controls breathing, and it is due to the slow response of the respiratory system to accommodate the suddenly imposed need for oxygen in the muscles. The anaerobic engine is required to help supply the energy until the aerobic engine gears itself to the pace. An oxygen debt is created and when it is repaid by the aerobic system, the athlete gets his "second wind". Thus, there is a real need for warming up prior to the start of the competition in order to begin sweating and to gear up the aerobic engine for the job at hand.

Oxygen Uptake Capacity

Oxygen uptake capacity is the measure of an individual's aerobic fitness; it is his ability to take in air, extract oxygen from the air, and transport it to the muscles doing the work. The maximal oxygen uptake is a measure of one's maximal energy output by aerobic processes. A high maximal oxygen uptake is desirable for all endurance athletes and especially for cross-country ski racers. If a skier attains a high maximal oxygen uptake, he can maintain a high speed for lengthy periods without going into costly anaerobic work except on uphills or during sprints. A skier with a lesser maximal oxygen uptake will require anaerobic work sooner at the same speed because his oxygen transport system cannot supply sufficient quantities of oxygen to support the aerobic engine discussed earlier . Thus he incurs an oxygen debt, lactic acid build-up in his muscles, and soon he must reduce his speed.

Each person is born with a unique potential aerobic power and only through training can one approach this potential. The length of time over which an athlete can work at close to his maximal oxygen uptake is also governed by the amount of training that he has done (see figure 7.1). Some top skiers have trained enough to be able to tap 85 per cent of their potential for long periods of work. But training can increase one's maximal aerobic power only 10 to 20 per cent. To get best results it is important to be very active between the ages of ten and twenty. During these years the necessary lung capacity and heart size can be developed so that one can later realize one's full aerobic potential. Thus, children should be included in competitive programs at an early age in order to build a solid base of ski racers later on.

Maximal oxygen uptake declines after age 20 to about 70 per cent of the original at about age 70. Nevertheless, best results in competition are usually obtained between ages 20 to 35 due to other variables such as increased muscle strength, technique, more experience, and motivation, all acquired after a number of years of training.

Factors Affecting Oxygen Uptake The value of one's maximal oxygen uptake ca-

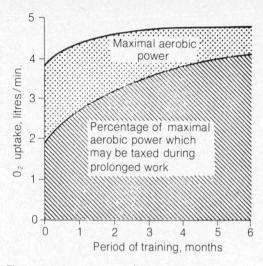

Figure 7.1:   Oxygen Uptake and Training

pacity depends mainly on the efficiency of two systems, the respiratory and circulatory systems. The respiratory system, the lungs, limits the volume of air that can be inhaled. This volume per breath is called the vital capacity. A large vital capacity, although advantageous, will certainly not alone produce a large maximal oxygen uptake. Not all of the oxygen breathed in is used, and only the amount that is withdrawn from the lungs and transported to the muscle cells governs the maximal oxygen uptake. Thus, the skier must have a well-developed cardio-vascular system, the system involving the heart, the blood, and the blood vessels.

Oxygen is absorbed in the lungs by the blood, especially by the hemoglobin in the red blood cells. It is then transported to the muscles where it is used in energy production. Waste products such as carbon dioxide are then carried away by the blood on its return trip to the lungs.

The blood is moved from the lungs to the muscles by the heart acting like a pump. The skier must have a high concentration of hemoglobin in his blood and a large, efficient heart to achieve maximal aerobic power. In the well-trained skier the resting heart rate will be slow (40 to 60 beats per minute), and the volume of blood pumped per beat (stroke volume) will be large, thus ensuring that maximal amounts of blood get to working muscles. In addition the well-trained skier has greater vascularization; that is, he has a greater network of blood vessels and capillaries through which oxygenated blood can be dispersed to the muscles. Thus, during exercise the trained person's heart need not beat so quickly as the untrained; because of its efficiency it can pump an equal amount of blood at this lower rate to an expanded circulatory system.

The heart rate can vary from about 40 to 200 beats per minute. Resting pulse rates for athletes vary from 40 to 60 beats per minute, and depending on the age of the person, maximum rates vary from about 160 to over 200 beats per minute for persons of 20 years or less. As one ages, his heart rate declines.

A high heart rate does not necessarily signify an efficient heart. Only when the stroke volume is also large, having been increased by training, does a high rate mean much more blood and oxygen for the muscles.

A good indication of cardio-vascular efficiency is the recovery rate of the heart after hard work. In the well-trained person the heart rate will return to normal much more quickly than in the untrained person after strenuous exercise.

Muscle Function

Muscles provide the skier with strength for speed and endurance. Muscle strength is required to achieve and maintain a fast tempo, to climb hills, and to maintain hard work for long periods.

The ratio of red to white fibres in the muscle will determine how well it will function for speed or endurance. A muscle containing more red fibres is better for endurance work. It contains large amounts of myoglobin, the oxygen container of the muscle. Muscles with predominantly red fibres are capable of many slow, powerful contractions and are not tired easily.

Muscles with predominantly white fibres, which have less myoglobin, are specialized for speed. They can contract quickly, but they tire easily in prolonged work.

The quantity and ratio of red to white fibres in the muscles in the body never changes from birth. Essentially one is born with the speed that he has throughout life. It is not possible to make a slow person fast, but it is possible to tone up muscles and muscle function in order to improve speed to some degree. With exercise the muscle fibres enlarge to become stronger and more efficient.

Through practice and training the muscular and nervous systems adjust to make complicated movements more efficient. During contraction the muscle tends to block blood flow so maximal muscle tension should be maintained for only a few seconds. After contraction, wastes of energy production and use must be washed away by the blood, and a relaxed muscle is necessary for this process. These facts point up the value of a good ski technique which combines explosive kicks followed by quick but relaxed returns. In every stride there must be a rest phase for these processes to operate efficiently. Hence, it is important to practise skiing until the neuromuscular function becomes well developed, that is, until the movements become smooth and automatic. Any skier who has a tense and tight technique, always fearful of losing his balance during each glide, will soon suffer exhaustion and the build-up of lactic acid in the muscles.

Strength may vary from day to day by as much as 10 to 20 per cent and maximal strength is achieved during the ages of 20 to 30. Declining with age, it becomes only 80 per cent of one's best at age 65. Women on the average have only two thirds the strength of men of equal age, children are also handicapped in that their size to strength ratio is low. Thus women and youngsters should not be forced to race men's distances nor should youngsters be forced into competing against adults.

The Energy Costs of Skiing

Cross-country skiing makes heavy demands on the large muscle groups over long periods; hence, energy costs are high. A skier working continuously for two and one half hours may burn up nearly 3000 Calories. Skiers racing the Vasaloppet Race in Sweden (a 53-mile course) have been known to expend 6000 to 7000 Calories of energy.

The greater the speed and the closer to maximal aerobic capacity the work intensity, the higher will be the energy demand. Earlier it was noted that the transport of oxygen to the muscles could limit the amount and rate of work possible. Similarly the stores of fuel in the muscles and the rate at which they are expended can also limit the amount and rate of work. For example, at a rate of 25 to 30 per cent of his maximal aerobic power, a person may be able to ski for 8 to 10 hours before the energy stores are exhausted. But at a rate of 75 to 80 per cent of maximal aerobic power, he may only be able to ski for 1 to 2 hours before his energy stores are

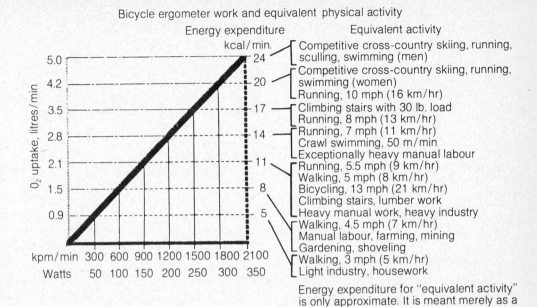

Bicycle ergometer work and equivalent physical activity

Energy expenditure
kcal/min.

Equivalent activity

24 — Competitive cross-country skiing, running, sculling, swimming (men)

20 — Competitive cross-country skiing, running, swimming (women)
Running, 10 mph (16 km/hr)

17 — Climbing stairs with 30 lb. load
Running, 8 mph (13 km/hr)

14 — Running, 7 mph (11 km/hr)
Crawl swimming, 50 m/min
Exceptionally heavy manual labour

11 — Running, 5.5 mph (9 km/hr)
Walking, 5 mph (8 km/hr)

8 — Bicycling, 13 mph (21 km/hr)
Climbing stairs, lumber work
Heavy manual work, heavy industry

5 — Walking, 4.5 mph (7 km/hr)
Manual labour, farming, mining
Gardening, shoveling
Walking, 3 mph (5 km/hr)
Light industry, housework

O₂ uptake, litres/min
5.0, 4.2, 3.5, 2.8, 2.1, 1.5, 0.9

kpm/min 300 600 900 1200 1500 1800 2100
Watts   50 100 150 200 250 300 350

Energy expenditure for "equivalent activity" is only approximate. It is meant merely as a general guide. It depends, among other things, on the weight of the subject. The examples listed are based on the average person with a body weight of 160 lb (70.75 kg)

Figure 7.2:   Energy Costs of Physical Activity

exhausted. Such extensive energy demands must be met by proper diet and by in-race nourishment.

The Fuel

The two fuels used to produce energy in the muscles are carbohydrates and fats. Both of these substances are eventually changed to glycogen, stored in the muscles, and to glucose, stored in the liver and blood. Glycogen and glucose fuel the muscles during work.

Carbohydrate foods tend to give better energy yields and it has been found that athletes can work three times as long on a high carbohydrate diet as on a high fat diet. Carbohydrate foods yield about 10 per cent more energy per litre of oxygen consumed than do fatty foods. In prolonged work, such

as that encountered in a 50-kilometre ski race, initially fat contributes only 25 to 30 per cent of the energy and carbohydrates the remainder, but as the race progresses and carbohydrate stores are depleted, fat stores contribute more to the energy requirements, up to 60 per cent. Thus it seems that carbohydrate foods are best for endurance work, but a totally carbohydrate diet is inadvisable in that fats and proteins are necessary for other body functions as well. On the basis of a 3000-Calorie-plus energy-expenditure per day, a good diet should contain amounts of protein, fat, and carbohydrate in the ratio of 1:1:4 respectively.

Vitamins are a classical ingredient in the diet of the athlete, but there is not yet sufficient evidence that they are necessary in amounts above those obtained in the normal, well-prepared diet. It takes a long time to incur a vitamin deficiency, and experiments have shown that even after one week without any vitamin intake, work capacity was not affected. Increased vitamin intake likewise has shown no effect on performance.

On the other hand, the intake of extra vitamins can do no harm and they may prove beneficial when one is travelling and normal food is not available. Overcooking often destroys vitamins in foods, especially vitamin C, and extra amounts ingested in concentrated form may well supplement some restaurant foods. By eating extra fruit, dairy products, green, leafy vegetables, and meat, one can ensure an adequate supply of vitamins and minerals necessary to sustain an active body.

Storage of Fuel　Fat is the most efficiently stored fuel in the body in that it is in concentrated form and requires little space. Carbohydrate, on the other hand, is stored with water, and thus the body cannot store great amounts. Carbohydrates are stored in modified form in the muscles, liver, and the blood.

For prolonged exercise and ski races of less than one hour's duration, this stored carbohydrate fuel is adequate to fuel the muscles, and it is only the maximal oxygen uptake that limits energy production. But for the longer events more fuel is required, and the less efficient fat must be used.

The initial glycogen content of the muscles seems to be very important in the ability of the athlete to perform for a long time. For example, if the initial energy stores in the muscles at the start of exercise are increased from say .6 per cent glycogen by weight to 1.75 per cent, the person is able to perform twice as long at a given high workload. Thus it is important to have as much glycogen stored in the muscles as possible when race day arrives, especially for long races.

Increasing the Fuel Storage　Because storage of large amounts of glycogen is of paramount importance for longer races, one must plan to try to maximize his carbohydrate stores prior to race day. This feat can be accomplished by again taking advantage of the body's ability to adapt to stress. Through a program designed to first deplete the carbohydrate or sugar stores and then to overfill them, one can fool the body into storing more than a normal amount of this fuel.

Three methods are possible to increase sugar stores and they are given in table 7.1.

Methods 2 and 3 should be used only prior to important and long races where one needs a large amount of fuel. In order to exhaust the sugar stores in the body the "hard skiing" in this table must be of fast tempo in fairly tough terrain to be sure that energy demands are great.

When energy stores get low, the skier becomes progressively more exhausted and sometimes somewhat light in the head. Co-ordination becomes worse, and with the appearance of these symptoms, the skier knows that he has exhausted his sugar stores. After the hard skiing session when he sits down to a supper of about 75 per cent carbohydrate foods, his body begins to adapt to the depletion by storing greater amounts of sugar as glycogen and glucose.

It is important to take care not to get caught a long way from home or food when exhaustion sets in. In such a state one can become cold easily, and the chance of frostbite is enhanced. It is best to practise the above techniques on a circular track of short enough length so that one is never too far from warm clothing or a warm building.

Food During the Race

In longer events the glycogen and glucose stores are often depleted before the finish,

Table 7.1   Schedule for overstoring carbohydrates

Method	Day 6	Day 5	Day 4	Day 3	Day 2	Day 1	Day of the Competition	Sugar storage weight%
1	Normal diet Normal training			High carbohydrate diet No training				1.75-2.5%
2	Normal diet Normal training		Hard skiing 1½ hrs.	High carbohydrate diet No training				3.5%
3	Hard skiing 1½ hrs.	High fat + protein diet Light training	Hard skiing 1½ hrs.	High carbohydrate diet No training				4.0+%

and it becomes necessary to take in extra sugar. The sugar can be taken in a solution with a sugar concentration of from 10 to 40 per cent at temperatures ranging from 70° to 80° F. If the sugar solution is too strong, it will tend to cause fluids to collect in the stomach to dilute the extreme concentration before it can be taken into the blood. Thus sugar ingested in tablet form or in other concentrated forms without liquid is not advisable, because it may cause stomach cramps or nausea. Also blood will necessarily be diverted away from the muscles to the stomach in larger than normal volumes to dilute the concentrated sugar. To get full benefit from drinking during the race and to minimize possible side effects, one should practise drinking sugared liquids during training sessions.

If sugared drink is not taken during long races, blood sugar levels begin to fall as the stores of glucose are exhausted. This decline affects the central nervous system and diverts blood away from the muscles to the brain which has priority on the remaining blood sugar. Thus, even though the muscles are capable of metabolizing glycogen, the ability for further work is limited by the decline of blood sugar. By ingesting sugared liquids early in the race, blood sugar levels are maintained and work can continue until muscle glycogen stores are near exhaustion.

Recipes for various sweet drinks and schedules for their intake are given later in chapters 8 and 9 respectively.

Water Balance

An athlete training in a temperate climate may lose up to five litres of water per day and this water must be replaced by the water from food and the water in liquid drinks. In long ski races, skiers may lose up to a litre of water per hour. This loss is essential

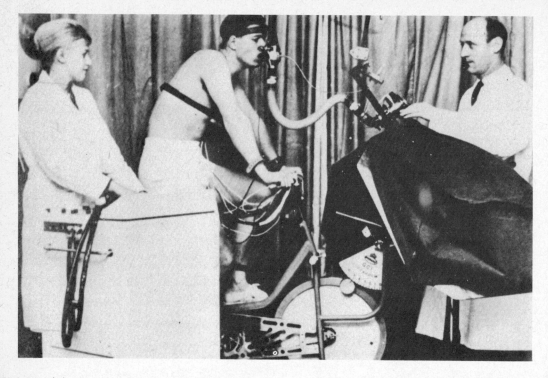

to cool the body which may produce ten to twenty times more heat than normal during heavy exercise.

Water is lost through perspiring and in exhaled air as water vapour. Not all the water that finds its way into the exhaled air is lost. Some is reclaimed by the mucous glands along with precious body heat, especially in very cold weather. Some is condensed in the nasal passages giving rise to the scourge of all cross-country skiers—the runny nose!

Loss of water can greatly affect athletic performance especially in the long-distance skiing events. A loss of 1 to 2 per cent of the body weight (0.6 to 0.9 litres) may lessen performance by as much as 5 to 10 per cent. After a water loss of 4 to 5 per cent of the body weight, aerobic work capacity can be decreased by as much as 30 to 40 per cent. Dehydration causes a

decrease in the heart rate, thus decreasing the normal efficiency of the heart.

Obviously, if one wishes to maintain top performance for as long as possible during a race, he must replace the water loss. In competitions of one hour's duration or less (15 kilometres or less) dehydration is not a serious problem, but in longer events it is necessary to begin to replace fluids early in the race before their loss begins to lower performance. Ordinarily water is replaced by periodic drinks of sugared liquid, which in addition to covering the water loss also provides sugar to replenish energy stores.

During water loss through perspiration, salt is also lost from the body in small amounts. Salt is necessary to maintain the water balance in the body. During competition it is not necessary to take in extra salt and a liberal sprinkling on meals should suffice to replace the losses incurred during training and racing. In competition one's water loss can be great and the concentration of salt in the blood becomes quite high. Thus there is no need to try to increase this concentration by ingesting more salt. Replacing the liquids is more important.

Tobacco and Alcohol

Without any doubt an athlete who must develop a high maximal aerobic capacity to perform well in his sport must not smoke. Cigarette smoke raises the level of carbon monoxide in the blood and this chemical tends to combine with hemoglobin, rendering it useless for transporting oxygen. Only 10 to 12 cigarettes per day can raise the carbon monoxide level in the blood to 5 per cent. Even though the body can tolerate levels to 10 per cent at rest, during physical work much lower levels will interfere with oxygen uptake capacity. Smoking may bring about a 5 to 10 per cent loss in aerobic power, and if one considers that training can increase the maximal aerobic power by only 10 to 20 per cent, then it is hardly wise to smoke and destroy 50 per cent of the physical build-up attained through hard training.

In addition to raising the heart rate, smoking also increases airway resistance in the throat and lungs. Smoke particles are undesirable materials in the respiratory system so the body reacts by increasing mucous production to protect lung tissues. This reduces gas exchange and the efficiency of the aerobic engine.

The use of alcohol by athletes has long been a very controversial topic. Physiologically there seems to be no harm in the use of alcohol in small quantities. It apparently has no effect on the maximal aerobic capacity of the individual, although if taken in excess, alcohol does cause dehydration and potassium depletion.

Potassium is an important mineral utilized primarily in the nervous system and also seems to be a factor in increasing endurance.

Large doses of alcohol also destroy neuromuscular co-ordination and are not recommended during competition. In fact, ingesting alcohol during a competition is considered to be a form of doping.

It has been the custom of some ski racers in long events to have a small amount of alcohol in their last drink before the finish to celebrate the end of the race. More than once this act has resulted in a chaotic last few kilometres. When one is in a state of dehydration and fatigue, the alcohol hits hard and fast.

The social aspects of alcohol use are probably more problematical than the actual use, in that alcohol is normally associated with late nights, crowded, smoky bars, and lack of care of the health. In all certainty, the athlete should avoid the use of alcohol in excessive quantities if he is seriously trying to excel at his sport.

Bibliography

Much of the factual information presented in this chapter has been taken from the following works. They offer a wealth of information and advice somewhat beyond the scope of this book, but they are recommended for the serious skier who wishes to know more about the physiology of training.

1. Astrand, P.O., and K. Rodahl. *Textbook of Work Physiology.* New York: McGraw-Hill, 1970.
2. Lydiard, A.L. *The How and Why of Middle Distance and Distance Running Training.* Berlin: Verlag Burtels and Wernitz, 1968.
3. Williams, J.G.P. *Medical Aspects of Sport and Physical Fitness.* London: Pergamon Press, 1965.

CHAPTER 8

Training and Conditioning

About Training

Training for ski racing events is geared to the integration of many factors. Cross-country ski racing is one of the most physically demanding of sports and athletic events. Competitors must have high maximal work capacities to achieve top results. They must train their bodies and muscles to efficiently use oxygen and sugar to produce energy. They must train to increase the capabilities of their lungs, heart, and circulatory system to take in and transport oxygen in large volumes to help fuel muscles over long periods of from twenty minutes to three hours. They must train their muscles to increase their strength and endurance.

In addition the cross-country ski competitor must practise to achieve an efficient, explosive ski technique. He must prepare himself mentally in order to sustain a high degree of motivation over the many months of training and preparation for just a few months of competition.

In order to increase the efficiency of the oxygen transport system and muscles, the skier must put these systems under stress through exercise or work. Each time they are stressed by physical training they adapt to make it easier for the next session. Hence over a long time, successive training sessions will elevate the ability of the athlete to perform at greater levels of stress for longer periods until he reaches his full potential of maximal aerobic and anaerobic power.

This chapter is devoted to the explanation of how one prepares physically and mentally for competition in cross-country skiing.

Level of Training

It is essential that demands be placed on the body systems in ever-increasing doses over a lengthy period. It is unwise for a novice to jump right into the training program of an Olympic athlete, because the body cannot adapt quickly enough and totally to such rigorous demands and generally the health gives way. One must be well trained to train well!

In considering a training program one must decide on the amount, intensity, and regularity of training. These factors should be determined to fit one's age and life style. Younger persons should train a lesser amount and at lower intensity than older persons who have already done a few years of training. If a skier is employed at manual labour in his occupation then he may need lesser amounts of training than a student who gets no physical training value from his work. It is very important to try to fit one's training into one's everyday life by scheduling time for other activities as well as training. Skiers who live only to train and ski tend to have a short-lived competitive life. They become so "saturated" with their sport that it becomes a burden rather than a challenge.

Regular Training

Regularity in training is important. Elite skiers train six to seven days per week throughout the year with only a little rest time in the spring. The amount and intensity of training will vary for each session and during the seasons of the year. Year round training keeps one at his top capacity for longer periods. The skier should set an initial program that he can complete without too much stress. After three to four weeks he can increase the amount and/or intensity to the next level until the training again becomes easy to handle. Initial improvement comes quickly and relatively easily, but the improvement needed to make the break through to the top is not easily acquired. One may have to add smaller increments to his training at this level so that the body will not be overtaxed.

Generally speaking, one is able to judge when to increase the training by the amount of fatigue incurred during his workout sessions and by the length of his recovery time. If recovery time from a tough workout is ten to twelve hours, he may move on to another level of training.

Training should be systematic; that is, it should be designed to put ever-increasing increments of stress onto the cardio-vascular and muscle systems. It should be well planned to train all aspects of the body needed to ski fast and long; hence, training should be planned and carried out towards a goal, whether it be a short term goal such as an important race one to two months hence or the Olympics four years hence.

Everyone is different physiologically and psychologically; therefore, it is necessary for the individual to select a program suited to his temperament, ability, and experience. Of course, one must follow the basic philosophy of training, but it is possible to adjust programs to suit the individual and still do productive training. Variety in training is sometimes necessary to maintain proper motivation and interest.

Training Goals

Anyone who decides to subject himself to a rigorous training program should do so with a goal in mind. Training for cross-country ski racing is very tough both physically and mentally and one should set short term and long term goals that can be eventually achieved. The realization of a personal goal such as cutting minutes off a racing time, beating faster opponents, skiing a technically perfect race, or making a national or international team is the reward that justifies training.

It is virtually impossible to keep top form

or condition year round; thus one must plan his training to build all systems to a physical peak for the time when they are most needed. Often elite racers will do relatively poorly in the early season races, but two months later they may win a national or a world championship race. Their win is no accident. They chose the big race as their goal and planned their training to reach optimum condition at the right moment. Whereas the short term goals are usually one or two races in the ski racing season, the long term goals may span several seasons. A person training to make an Olympic team, for example, will plan his yearly training to increase over a span of three or four years and will set a goal to be in his best condition ever for the trial races and the Olympic events.

Whether the goal lies three weeks, three months, or three years in the future one should always plan his training and skiing around his life-style. Training hard in the fall is very tough when one is not sure whether his job or other commitments will allow him to race in the winter. Such speculative training is mentally depressing and can do more to destroy enthusiasm than all of the physical rigors of the training itself. Not only should one plan to achieve a certain goal, but he must also arrange his life and business to make the way clear to realizing it.

Training Diary

In order to be able to evaluate the effect and success of training, one should keep a diary of the amounts and types of training he does over the seasons and the years. After a season of training and racing, one can review his training and make adjustments to improve next year's results. The format of the diary may take the form of the example given in table 8.1.

Table 8.1   Training Diary

Month	Day	Rest pulse A.M.	Weight A.M.	Pulse return time	Distance training		Interval training		Tempo training		Roller skiing		Weight training		Competition	Daily totals		Remarks
		b/min.	lbs.	hr.	hr.	km	hr.	km	hr.	km	hr.	km	hr.	km	time	hr.	km	
																		←Monthly totals

Summary

1. Total training before this month

2. Total training for this month

3. Total training for this year

	Kms	Hours	Days

Types of Training

Without a doubt the best training for skiing is to ski, but one must also carry on other types of training during the snowless months of the year. This "dryland" training is made up of exercises and training routines which are as close to the motions of skiing as possible. Thus a good dryland training program will condition the oxygen transport system (aerobic engine), the ability to withstand lactic acid build-up or oxygen debt (the anaerobic engine), and muscular strength required for skiing. These requirements can be met through a well-integrated program of distance, interval, oxygen debt (tempo), and specific strength training.

Distance Training

Distance training is one of the most important types of training for the cross-country ski racer. Reasonably good race results can be achieved through a distance program alone, but the same results can not be obtained through a program of interval and strength training alone.

The principle behind distance training is to run or ski for long distances and hence subject the body to lengthy periods of constant stress to build up endurance. Normally maximal amounts of this type of training are carried out in the summer and early fall months to provide a training base for subsequent interval and oxygen debt training.

It is important to build the aerobic condition in order to be able to cover long distances in a nearly tireless state without creating large oxygen debts and to be able to recover quickly. In other words distance training should be carried out aerobically so there is no significant build-up of lactic acids and so that one can recover quickly enough to continue training next day.

Dryland training

Not everyone is capable of putting on a pair of shoes or skis and running or skiing for three to four hours in their first try. You must test yourself to determine your capabilities and thus your initial work load by running or skiing out a trail or road for fifteen to thirty minutes; if you take longer to return, then the pace is too great for your present state of aerobic efficiency. By adjusting the pace, you will be able to carry on for the whole distance at a constant speed. It is the speed that limits performance by the build-up of oxygen debts, not the distance; therefore, initially it is wise to go slowly and ignore your speed. If you have done your distance training properly then you should feel tired at the end but at the same time feel that you could have run faster.

Ski striding with poles

Methods of Distance Training Dryland distance training should simulate skiing as much as possible in terms of movements.

Many skiers train by running for three to four hours on flat roads. This in itself is not enough because skiing requires the training of the large muscle groups. In order to benefit maximally from your aerobic training, you must get as many muscles into operation as possible.

One method is to select a training area that is quite hilly. You will build the leg muscles during aerobic distance training if you ski stride or bound up the hills with complete rearward leg extension as in skiing. Better still is to carry ski poles and use them as you would in skiing. This type of ski striding also brings the upper body into motion. By poling and ski striding along flats and uphills as you would in skiing, you can train specific muscle function as well as aerobic capacity.

By using both your upper body and lower body you may find that you will have to reduce speed compared to your normal running speed in order to cover the same distance. Do not be alarmed; you are still taxing the aerobic capacity to the same extent by using more muscles and at the same time you are conditioning the upper body.

Other forms of exercise can be used for endurance training as well. Cycling, canoeing, rowing, fast walking, and hiking in mountains for long periods are but a few of the many forms of endurance training. Keep in mind though that the exercise that involves many large muscle groups and that requires the body to move itself continuously against gravity is the best and will require the least time to generate aerobic conditioning. Thus ski striding or running will be more beneficial than an activity such as swimming where the body is supported by flotation.

Nevertheless, just jogging around is not sufficient. You must exert a constant stress on the respiratory and cardiovascular systems to produce the training effect. A general rule is to keep the heart rate above 120 beats per minute, preferably at 130 to 140 beats per minute.

As you become capable of handling a specific distance, you can increase the distance or increase the speed or tempo over the same distance in order to increase the work load. Aerobic condition builds up fairly quickly, and you will soon be able to cover long distances at slow speeds.

The body becomes used to work over long periods and psychologically one feels fit and comfortable. Distance training builds confidence. After completing a good distance program, you know that you have built the necessary stamina to push through the long distances of cross-country ski-racing events. You should aim to train over distances one and a half to two times the length of the races you intend to enter. Therefore, for a 15 kilometre event, you should prepare with distance sessions of 20 to 30 kilometres at least.

Interval Training

Interval training consists of intermittent work periods separated by rest periods of reduced activity. It is designed to stress the aerobic engine through repetition of near maximal efforts and is thus more psychologically demanding than distance training.

The principle involved is to cover short distances at high speed in order to introduce high oxygen demand but not to the point where the anaerobic processes take over. The work may last from 30 seconds to 10 minutes without incurring significant oxygen debt depending on the initial condition of the athlete.

After the work period a rest is necessary for muscles to recover so that successive intervals will not produce an increasing oxygen debt. Usually the rest intervals are at least as long as the work intervals and a good guide is to rest until the heart rate drops again to 120 beats per minute.

The intensity of the work intervals should be from 80 to 100 per cent of one's aerobic capacity and a fair judge of this level is a heart rate of about 10 to 15 beats below maximum. Any increased work above this level is likely to be anaerobic and will not contribute to the development of the aerobic engine.

Thus when beginning to do interval training you should determine how long a maximal work period you can withstand and still recover to 120 beats per minute heart rate in 2 to 3 minutes. This work period will be your starting work interval from which you can increase as your recovery times become less.

Again it is important in interval training not to incur large oxygen debts; that is, do not carry on the work interval until the muscles become stiff. Once in this state the muscles may become unable to perform to an extent where the oxygen transport system is sufficiently stressed and you will have to cut short the work early.

During rest intervals one should keep moving at about 40 per cent effort to speed up recovery. Relaxed muscle motion helps the blood to circulate and "wash" away the metabolites produced during the hard work. Even during this rest phase the oxygen transport system is being stressed as these processes are operating.

Methods of Interval Training Interval training can be conducted systematically by doing repetitions in a reasonably steep uphill or it can be done as a natural interval during a distance session by the insertion of occasional hard, fast sprints where the terrain offers sufficient resistance. For effective, systematic interval training, the length of the work intervals should be varied to condition the body to perform at near maximum for different durations. Short, intense interval sprints of 15 to 60 seconds should be interspersed with long sprints of 3 to 10 minutes. An example of a good system, performed on a lengthy, steep upgrade is outlined below.

> 3 x 3 minutes
> 3 x 1 minute
> 3 x 30 seconds

By completing the longer intervals first and the shorter ones later, one can maintain mental enthusiasm throughout such a demanding workout. When each subsequent set of intervals is made shorter, it becomes psychologically easier to do them at high intensity. Also one is fresher for the longer intervals and can do them with proper technique and speed.

The work load must be great for interval training and three means exist to regulate it. One is to vary speed, one is to vary the slope of the running or ski track, and the third involves varying the duration of the work interval. Thus to increase the intensity of interval work, one can either increase the speed, increase the length of the work interval, shorten the rest interval, or seek a hill with a steeper gradient. The interval hill should be gentle enough to afford good footing or purchase but steep enough to provide good resistance.

To get the maximum effect in dryland intervals, ski poles should be used to engage the muscles of the upper body as well as the legs. One should bound up the hill, springing forward from a bent knee and ending with full leg and arm extension in the same manner as skiing. This exercise offers an unlimited resistance. One can make it as tough or as easy as he needs. When interval training is carried out on skis, the same basic principles hold true.

For interval training on skis one should prepare an interval loop with an uphill of

Dryland Intervals: The photo shows the proper ski-striding technique for uphill work—a good extension of the arms and legs and a good high bounce

steady gradient and an easy downhill return. The hill should not be so steep as to require the herringbone, but should allow one to ski up with a fast diagonal all the while sliding the skis. In addition the track must be hard packed and well prepared to allow for fast skiing without the need for dodging obstructions or sinking into soft snow. To ski fast in the race one must ski fast in training!

Distance or Interval Training?

Some coaches argue for greater amounts of interval as opposed to greater amounts of distance training for the long distance athlete. Theoretically and physiologically, interval training produces the same result as distance training in a shorter but more intense work period (i.e., one hour of interval training may have only twenty minutes of actual work) but there are some dangers involved.

In the first place, it takes a highly motivated individual to carry through an entirely interval training program because it is very hard to maintain psychologically. Secondly, few persons have a very accurate knowledge of their own capabilities to know exactly when they must cut off the work interval to prevent anaerobic processes from operating. The build-up of lactic acid from such intensive training day after day can increase the acidity of the blood interfering with the work of vitamins and enzymes. The capacity to recover from training is reduced and eventually acid build-up interferes with neuro-muscular function to produce staleness, irritability, and lack of interest.

On the other hand, distance training can be pleasant and challenging providing a steady, sustained pressure on the aerobic system without the by-products of anaerobic work; hence, recovery can be quick and complete. The only drawback is that distance training requires more time.

In reality, a training program must incorporate both types. Thus distance training provides an endurance base on which to build the speed from interval and tempo training. The proportion of each will be determined by the skier's goals and motivation, but as a general rule the program should include roughly a 3:2 ratio of distance to interval respectively in terms of hours of training.

Tempo or Oxygen Debt Training

Tempo training, often called oxygen debt training, prepares the skier to maintain the speed required during a race. The object is to either run or ski at maximal speed for a period equal to 10 to 20 per cent of the race duration. Thus the work periods last for 5 to 30 minutes separated by periods of rest. For example, in one workout you might do four work periods of 5 minutes, or three of 10 minutes, and so on depending on your capacity and condition.

Tempo training by its very nature will produce an oxygen debt as work periods become faster and longer. Thus tempo training is also geared to increase your tolerance to high lactic acid levels produced during maximal, anaerobic work. That is, it prepares you to be able to go all out in sprinting hills and maintaining high speeds for lengthy periods. The idea is to push yourself until the muscles become stiff and further work is impossible, then to rest and repeat as many times as one can stand.

This type of training is the most demanding, physiologically and psychologically, and you should be careful to select a program which fits your capacity. If you are in your first year of intensive training you should shorten the length of maximal work to 30 to 60 seconds, but if more experienced you may choose periods of 5 minutes or more.

Methods of Tempo Training

Dryland oxygen debt training can consist of any of the methods used for interval training extended to maximal effort. Ski striding with poles is again probably the best type of activity for tempo training because it places the greatest demands on the greatest number of muscles.

On skis, one should select a hilly section of well-packed trail and sprint at full speed until the muscles become unresponsive and technique breaks down. After a rest of easy skiing, one can repeat the process as often as possible.

Tempo training is usually left out of the program until late fall or early winter. Only after a full season of training and physical build-up is one in a position to practise skiing or moving quickly over longer distances. It is necessary to build strength and endurance first, then to add the speed.

Muscle Training

Muscle training must accomplish two things. It should strengthen muscles and it should produce supple and quick muscles. These requirements can be met through a program of specific muscle training designed to train only the skiing muscles. There is no advantage to carrying around extra, heavy, large muscle groups which are of no use in skiing.

Building Strength

Strength is an important ingredient for the cross-country ski racer and is especially needed to perform well in heavy, wet conditions or in rugged terrain. Strength training, therefore, should be an integral part of the general training program and the required amount and intensity of this type of training will necessarily vary among individuals. For example, an office clerk will need to build more strength training into his program than will a bushworker to achieve the same results.

Strength training comprises a series of exercises that offer high resistance to certain skiing muscle groups. The resistances can be artificial in the form of weights or natural in the form of moving the body weight against gravity. Most cross-country skiers prefer to use the body and the terrain to provide natural resistance for their strength training.

In laying out a program, determine the muscles that require extra training (usually the upper body) and then try several upper body exercises to find out the maximum number of times that you can perform them. In each training set (series of exercises), you should do only one half this maximum for each exercise in the set. The sets can be repeated several times and interspersed with rest periods until you are tired. Each month you must test yourself to determine new maximums for each exercise and adjust your program accordingly.

Methods of Strength Training *Leg Strength.* Leg strength can be trained effectively during aerobic or tempo training as outlined earlier, through the selection of demanding terrain with many uphill sections. By ski striding with bounding strides on these uphills during distance or interval work, you can build leg strength at the same time. Be sure to practise full extension of the legs and push off each step to simulate the kick in striding. In this manner you will be training specific skiing muscles in the thighs and calves.

Artificial resistance can be generated by a series of exercises using weights or other mechanical means. With weights on the shoulders equalling 40 per cent of the body weight, you can jump up and down, bouncing off the toes and sinking in the knees on landing, or you can do squats with an explosive extension (see figure 8.1). When working with weights it is wise to keep the movements quick and the weights relatively small. The idea is to build strength, but at the same time train the muscles to react quickly.

Rope skipping is another exercise that can build up the legs; if done long and fast

Figure 8.1

enough, it can also provide aerobic training. Other non specific but related strength training for the legs can be done by cycling or playing field games like soccer.

Arm Strength. Arm strength can be trained naturally by employing ski poles and arm action during dryland interval or tempo training on uphill work. In recent years roller skiing has come in vogue for training the upper body. By double poling along flat and gentle inclines on these devices, you can train the upper body, especially the triceps of the upper arm and the shoulders, exactly as you would with skis on the snow. Diagonal technique can be used if you select an unpaved road where the skis do not roll too easily and the speed is slow enough. Usually the skis roll too fast on hard surfaces to employ proper diagonal. The degree of resistance provided by this exercise can be varied by selecting rougher surfaces and steeper uphills.

Exercises with weights and pulleys can also serve to train upper body muscle strength as shown below in figure 8.2. By bending over at the waist, drawing weights up to the chest, and slowly returning them to their initial position, you can build up the triceps as well as the back. By using rubber bands or weighted pulleys as in figure 8.3 below and by pulling with the arms with a skiing-like rhythm, you can also train the arms. Other related exercises which provide training for the skiing muscles of the upper body can include push-ups, rowing, paddling, digging, chopping, and other forms of manual labour.

Body Strength. Other muscle groups that provide power and strength in skiing are the abdominal muscles and back muscles. It is necessary to train the strength of these muscles as well as those of legs, shoulders, and arms. The weakest of the muscle groups used for skiing will determine the limits of performance; thus, there is no sense in training the legs to great strength if the arms or stomach are not equally strong enough to sustain the output of the legs.

The best exercises for the stomach muscles are sit-ups and leg-raises for the upper and lower abdominal muscles respectively. Sit-ups should be practised with bent knees and a twist of the body with each raise from the floor as shown in figure 8.4. Weights can be held behind the head

Figure 8.2

Figure 8.3

Figure 8.4

or on the chest to provide additional resistance. Leg-raises should be done with one leg at a time. While lying on the back, one can lift one leg straight up at a 90° angle to the body, press the back flat onto the floor, and then lift the other leg 6 to 12 inches up and rotate it. After several rotations the sequence can be shifted to the other leg.

For the back muscles one can do back arches from a prone position on the floor raising both the feet and head off the floor at the same time. Another exercise involves placing weights behind the neck on the shoulders and then bending over at the waist from a standing position and returning to the upright position. Care must be taken with this not to try too much weight in the beginning because the back is one of the most problematical areas of the human body and can be injured and aggravated very easily through overload.

Intensity and Duration of Strength Training It is important to keep in mind the objective of strength training for skiing. One must build strength for both speed and endurance to perform in skiing events; so it is necessary to build into a strength-training program opportunities to practise both these aspects.

Strength exercises, whether they are done with weights, rubber bands, roller skis, or in natural fashion, should incorporate the principles of interval and endurance train-

ing. That is, exercising should include sessions of fast, short repetitions at maximal output and sessions of lesser output but of longer duration. In this way the upper body muscles can be trained to accommodate the conditions of ski racing just as are the lower body muscles during the training of the cardiovascular system mentioned earlier.

Stretching Exercises

All of the exercises mentioned thus far are primarily designed to increase strength through many repetitions of muscle contraction. These exercises tend to shorten the muscles and slow them down. Therefore, it is necessary to include, preferably after strength training, a series of loosening or stretching exercises to limber up.

Lower Body Several good exercises are available for the lower body. Thigh muscles

Figure 8.5

can be stretched by standing on one foot and by pulling the other foot and heel tight up against the rump or by bending at the waist, grabbing the ankles, and pulling the upper body down towards the knees while keeping them straight. Thighs can also be stretched by extending the arms straight out in front of the body and kicking up towards the hands with a straight leg with each foot in turn. Another good exercise is to scissor jump on the spot to simulate ski striding with a loose but quick alternation of leg and arm extensions.

Hips can be loosened by standing with hands on hips, legs apart, and loosely rotating them in small circles in alternating directions. The knee and ankle joints can also be loosened by rotating the lower leg and foot respectively as shown in figure 8.5.

Ankles can also be stretched by leaning the face forward with the palms on a wall and pushing back onto the ankle through an over extended knee. These exercises are all illustrated in figure 8.5.

Upper Body   One of the best stretching exercises for the upper body is to hang from rings or a cross pole by the arms and twist the body from side to side or in a circle. This exercise also stretches muscles in the trunk and to some degree in the lower body as well. Other upper body exercises include loose stride jumping, cross-toe touching, and the relaxed breathing exercise. Cross-toe touching is done from a standing position with legs apart and hands raised above the head, from where they can alternately touch the opposing toes by a bending of the waist.

The breathing exercise is carried out by stretching the arms above the head, arching the back, and inhaling as much air as possible. This is then followed by a bending forward at the waist to allow the upper body to more or less "hang" from the

Figure 8.6

Arm-training with rubber bands. Note that the bands are attached high enough so that the pull is down and then back

hips and a complete, forced exhaling of air in the lungs. Not only does this exercise relax the upper body, but it also forces carbon dioxide out of the lungs and therefore is a very good exercise to speed recovery after a hard interval or tempo session.

Training Programs

It has already been mentioned that training should be systematic and should slowly build your physical and psychological strength for cross-country ski competition. The way in which it is easiest to realize these two aspects is to establish a training program; that is, lay down or plan a daily, weekly, monthly, and yearly series of training sessions designed to prepare you for racing.

Before establishing the program you must consider several factors and answer some pertinent questions. For example, do you have a suitable training site and do you have the time to carry out an extensive program? Are you willing to dedicate yourself to a gruelling program? What are your goals and are they worth the work required to achieve them? In addition, if you have racing experience you must come to realize your weak points and adjust your program to work more on them. By answering the above questions you will be able to begin to design a program to fit your life style, ambitions, and training environment.

The training program for skiing varies in intensity and character over the year. Basically it is divided into dryland, transitional, and ski-training sections. The amounts and types of training and their variation over the year are given in figure 8.7.

Dryland Training The dryland section is the longest, extending from late April to the end of November for the most of North America, and it is the period of most extensive work. Training intensity in the dryland period begins with light work in spring consisting of easy distance training; it progresses into tougher work during summer and early fall with a greater diet of interval training and in the late fall by the addition of tempo sessions. The maximum amounts and intensities of training for the

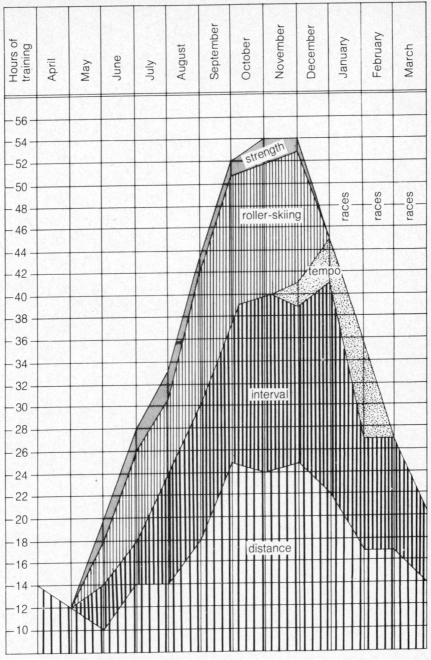

Figure 8.7: The Training Year

Table 8.2 Dryland Training

DAY	MAY	JUNE	JULY	AUG.	SEPT.	OCT.	NOV.
1	D—1½*	D—2½	D—2½	D—2½	D—3	D—3	D—3
2		NI—1 RS—1	NI—1½ RS—¾	NI—1 RS—¾	NI—1 RS—1	NI—1¼ RS—1¼	NI—1½ RS—1
3	EI—1 RS—1			D—2 AP—½	D—2 AP—¼	D—1½ RS—1	D—1¾ RS—1
4		D—1 RS—1	D—1 RS—1	LI—1¼ RS—½	LI—1 RS—1	IOD—1½	LIS—1½
5	D—1 AP—½			NI—1 AP—¼	D—1¼ I—¼	FD—1½ AP—½	FD—1½ RS—1
6		AP—½	LI—1 AP—½	RS—1½	NI—1¼ RS—1	LI—1¼ RS—¾	I+OD—1 AP—¼
7							

	Per Wk.	Per Mon.	Per Wk.	Per Mon.	Per Wk.	Per Mon.	Per Wk.	Per Mon.	Per Wk.	Per Mon.	Per Wk.	Per Mon.	Per Wk.	Per Mon.
D	2½	10	3½	14	3½	14	4½	18	6¼	25	6	24	6¼	25
I	1	4	1	4	2⅛	10	3¼	13	3½	14	4	16	3½	14
OD	0	0	0	0	0	0	0	0	0	0			½	2
T	0	0	0	0										
RS	1	4	2	8	1¾	7	2¾	11	3	12	3	12	3	12
AP	½	2	½	2	½	2	¾	3	¼	1	½	2	¼	1
	5	20	7	28	8¼	33	11¼	45	13	52	13½	54	13½	54

D = Distance
FD = Fast Distance
EI = Easy Interval
I = Interval
LI = Long Interval
NI = Natural Interval

LIS = Long Interval with Ski Poles
IOD = Interval Nearly OD
RS = Roller Skis
AP = Arm Pulleys
OD = Oxygen Debt

*Training is in units of hours.

year are done in late fall prior to the coming of the snow.

An example of such a program is given in table 8.2. The program is one designed for elite ski racers of some experience so that it will be necessary to modify it if you are a beginner or if you do not care to dedicate the amount of time it suggests. A good guide for adjustment is to reduce the types of training proportionately; in other words, keep the same ratio of hours to distance to interval and so on. Do not try to carry out the program if you have not trained before. Start easily by taking only one quarter or one third of the amounts suggested or insert additional rest days on which you can recover.

Do not worry about how far you go in the times suggested in the program. Begin by setting a pace for which you know that you can put in the required hours. As your condition improves, then you will cover more distance in the same time and automatically your training intensity rises.

Transitional Training With the arrival of the snow, training intensity drops and a few weeks of easy distance skiing with minor amounts of interval on foot allow one to make the transition to skiing once more. It is also important during this phase of training to concentrate on style and technique of skiing. You should try to develop good rhythm and balance through skiing as much as possible at an easy pace over moderately difficult terrain. If needed, skiing without poles can be included to improve your balance.

A rigorous, set program is virtually impossible to devise for this period because the training depends on the arrival and durability of the first snow. Nevertheless a guide program is listed in table 8.3.

Another transition period occurs in April at the end of the racing season and with the disappearance of the snow. During this time it is necessary to ease yourself into working out on foot again. It is best to take a two-week rest and begin easily on the softest terrain available until the muscles adjust to the motions of running and ski striding again. Once adjusted you can begin the dryland program as outlined for May.

Ski Training Ski training proper begins after the transition period and when the snow is reliable. It is characterized by an increased volume of tempo training in preparation for racing conditions. Amounts and types of training throughout the racing season will vary with the number and length of races that you enter. Races themselves provide the best tempo training so that during the week you should perhaps concentrate on interval and distance work. It is wise to get in at least one long workout during each week to keep up endurance. A diet of only interval training and racing is not sufficient to keep up strength and endurance over the whole winter season.

Table 8.3 Transition Training

Day	Training	Hours
1.	Distance—easy skiing in gentle terrain	2
2.	Distance—easy skiing in gentle terrain	1½
3.	(a) Distance—easy skiing in gentle terrain	1¼
	(b) Light interval on foot	¾
4.	Distance—easy skiing in gentle terrain	3
5.	(a) Distance—easy skiing in gentle terrain	1¼
	(b) Light interval on foot	¾
6.	Distance—easy skiing in gentle terrain	2½
7.	Rest	

2-3 weeks duration

On the whole training during the racing season should be geared towards eliminating weaknesses. If you are slow but have endurance, then work on interval and tempo, and if you are speedy but tire quickly, work on distance training.

An outline of a possible program is given in table 8.4 below. Adjust it to suit your needs and goals.

Table 8.4   Ski Training

Day	Dec.	Jan.	Feb. Mar. Apr.	
1	NI -1½	R-1	Same as	Same
2	D -3	LI/NI-1½	January.	as
3	NI -1¾	D-2½	Races can	May
4	I/T-1	T/R*-1¼	replace	
5	D -2½	D-1¾	Tempo or	
6	NI -1½	LI-1	O.D.	
7	D -Optional			

	Per Wk.	Per Mon.	Per Wk.	Per Mon.
D	5½	22	4¼	17
I	4¾	19	2½	10
T	1	4	2¼	9
	11¼	45	9	36

*R=race.

Training for the Tourer

In order to be able to enjoy the full season from the early snow to the April corn, the ski tourer might take a little from this chapter as well and do some conditioning for the early season. Surely it is not necessary to do intensive interval and tempo work just to go ski touring, but some pre-season endurance work will make the first of the ski season seem easy. Such training can take the form of walking, hiking, bicycling, jogging, or even easy ski striding. A little training is certainly beneficial for a total enjoyment of cross-country skiing, since the very technique of the sport requires a certain amount of physical fitness.

Psychological Factors in Training

A training program must not only produce increased physical capacity but it must also build a positive desire for skiing and racing. It must provide that necessary spark required to dash up hills with spirit and buoyancy. Thus the training program should also be psychologically sound. As long as training and competing are fun and offer a challenge, then your program is good; but if these functions become a chore then something is wrong.

Possibly your sport is no longer in harmony with your personal life—studies, work, and family. If this is the case then you must make adjustments by rescheduling or cutting down training. If there are too many conflicts with training, then you will soon be questioning the value of training and competing. Under this type of duress your race results soon become poor and your mental attitude falls even further.

To continue competing under this type of mental depression is not wise. If you find yourself in this situation, it is best to discontinue racing for a time and do some easy distance training to try to regain the feeling of enjoyment that you got from skiing before. After a week or two of this therapeutic skiing and assessment of your problem, you will again be ready to tackle the race track.

Cross-country ski racing requires year-round training, which means up to eight months of training for only four months of racing. Because one often gets mentally exhausted long before he becomes physically exhausted, it is necessary to arrange a training program with some flexibility to prevent boredom and mental fatigue.

Rollerskiing is an excellent way to train the upper body. Note that the technique of rollerskiing is similar to skiing itself

The training program should provide some variety. For example, a long bicycle tour could replace a distance training session on foot or a row across the lake could suffice as strength training. Canoe trips and camping trips with lots of paddling and por-taging offer excellent means of training with a difference. Keep in mind though that the bulk of training must be systematic and the variations presented above are but breaks to rejuvenate the motivation.

Aside from program changes, it is also a good idea to vary the training terrain or locale periodically to prevent boredom. Visit a friend who is also training and train with him, compare notes and talk about skiing and training—but do not let the training become a competition.

During the many months of training prior to snow, it is advisable to set minor training goals like completing a certrain distance or training trail in a certain time or working up to a certain number of repetitions on the interval hill. In this respect it is good to keep a diary so that you can refer back to your start and check your progress as the months pass. The more hours and kilometres that you pile up, the more confident and motivated you become. You know that you have done the work in training and feel confident that you will be able to hold your own on the race track. Without this confidence in your training program, you can not possibly perform your best. You will always be wondering if the training is proper or worth it.

Rest must be an active part of your training program. The objective of training is to build up the physical and mental capacities for racing, not to tear them down through excessive and unplanned training. Overtraining is a real danger and can cause neuromuscular breakdown and psychological depression as mentioned earlier; thus, it is wise to build rest days into the program to allow the body to recover and rebuild, especially after the most strenuous sessions. Do not fool yourself though: a break in training longer than two days is backslipping.

The mental stresses of training for cross-country skiing are reasonably great. A large amount of work must be done and much time invested over the months and even years needed to prepare. There is always the fear that after all this preparation one will not succeed because of poor wax, a broken ski, or sickness. Thus the program for training, although directed towards achieving skiing goals, should also be interesting and enjoyable for its own sake. Only in this manner can it foster and maintain year long motivation.

The one-step double pole can be used for variation

Roller skis

Testing Training Progress

There are several ways by which one can test his training progress and evaluate his condition. Basically they can be divided into laboratory and non-laboratory tests. The first group includes tests done in the laboratory and are available at most major universities, which incidentally, are anxious to have the opportunity to test skiers. The second group includes tests that can be conducted in the field without sophisticated equipment; hence, they are probably the best for the average individual.

Once or twice per month you can ski or run over a track of known distance and record your time. By comparing times over the same track under the same conditions after each month of training you can chart your progress.

With adequate and proper training the rest pulse rate goes down and this fact provides another easy test. By checking the rest pulse at the same time each day, usually before sleep at night or rising in the morning, and recording it, one can see whether his condition is improving.

Similarly the speed with which the pulse rate returns to normal after exercise is an indicator of condition. For example, immediately after an interval session the pulse rate may be as high as 180 beats per minute. If it returns to 100 to 120 beats per minute in two to three minutes then you are in reasonably good condition. By evening four to five hours later, the resting rate should be back to a normal of forty to sixty beats per minute. If the heart rate fails to return to normal by the next day you are most likely training much too hard for your present condition. You are not fully recovering and should ease up on either the intensity or amount of training.

Generally one can feel the condition improve. A willingness and eagerness to train, a good feeling, good appetite, and restful sleep are all indications of improved condition and a proper training load.

Conditioning can be evaluated quantitatively only in the laboratory by using a treadmill or a bicycle ergometer as the work load and by monitoring heart rate and expired air to determine a person's maximal oxygen uptake. The athlete is subjected to sequential increases in work load until further increases do not significantly raise his oxygen uptake. At this point he has reached his maximum ability to use oxygen. As mentioned in the last chapter, training can increase the maximal oxygen uptake so by periodically taking the treadmill or ergometer test the skier can chart improvements in conditioning.

It is not always necessary to work to maximum to determine the degree of fitness in the laboratory. Sub maximal tests can be performed on the bicycle ergometer measuring only the heart rate for a specific work load over a specific time. The heart rate is then matched to tables which predict the maximal oxygen uptake of the athlete. This test can be done because of the direct linear relationship between heart rate and maximal oxygen uptake.

There are problems with the accuracy of these tests however, because heart rates vary with age and also with individuals. Nevertheless, the technique is inexpensive and simple and can be used in a general evaluation of one's progress in training.

Care must be exercised when such scores are compared from one athlete to another or used to predict performance in a sport such as skiing. Other factors such as motivation, overall muscle strength, technical prowess, and experience all play important roles in determining performance. Physiological testing can be used to separate out obviously poorly conditioned skiers in a group, but a training race will do the same. Thus far the ski race itself is still the best selection device for determining who the best skiers are.

CHAPTER 9

Racing
Know-How

Cross-country skiers of many years experience will not always be able to make the transition from tourist to racer. In addition to being in good condition and having mastered the basics of waxing and technique, one should also know something about the technical refinements, preparations, and strategies needed for good race performance. Much of this is best learned through experience on the track and in races, but by way of introduction some of the elements of cross-country ski-racing are presented in the following sections.

Technique and Tempo

To be a proficient racer, one must have easily at his command all of the technical maneuvers explained in chapter three. Through an extensive training and coaching program, he must build the strength and skill necessary to ski fast with an explosive and automatic technique. The difference between touring and racing lies only in the speed of skiing, commonly referred to as tempo. Tempo involves two things: the frequency and the amplitude of the kick-glide sequence. To increase tempo one must increase both frequency and amplitude; that is, he must kick more often and harder to achieve a very high skiing tempo.

The Diagonal   Increased tempo requires some modification of technique to accommodate the faster movement of limbs. In the diagonal stride, with the emphasis on producing forward motion, the arms and legs must be fully extended front and rear. The poles and skis must be thrust forward in an aggressive reaching motion after each kick. One must concentrate on reaching out with the arms; the legs will automatically extend in phase with the

arms. A high tempo does not allow time for the slow pendulum-like return of the kicking leg and pushing arm as in touring.

Even though the return of the leg and arm is aggressive, it should not be stiff and awkward. It should start as a natural swing helped by the muscles. It then becomes an explosive or ballistic motion as the initial muscle contraction sets the limbs into their forward swing. After this the muscles relax, letting momentum do the rest. In this manner, the necessary small rest phase after each kick is still maintained.

Body Position   The racer must assume a neutral body position, with his central axis between the skis, from which he can transfer his weight completely and quickly from one ski to the other through the kick. The hips rotate loosely, in symmetry with the kick-glide sequence, but do not move laterally from the central axis.

Ski poles must be planted as close to the skis as possible; the arms are close to the body and pushed straight back. On the forward swing, the poles should be extended straight forward and should not be drawn in over the skis by a crooked elbow before being planted. Such a motion, usually the result of too much hip and body rotation, tends to cause the skier to push laterally when the pole is planted.

The Double Pole   The racer must use the double pole under faster conditions and therefore must modify it somewhat so that excessive speed does not carry him past his poles before he can push on them. Basically all he does is plant the poles earlier by over-extending his arms and thrusting his upper body forward. Then he draws himself forward onto the poles to the position where he can push to full extension.

Odd Martinsen of Norway—a master technician

Explosive kicks and full extensions equal high tempo

Again, there is not enough time to allow the body weight to "fall" on the poles to begin the push forward.

The finish of the double pole must be explosive, forcing the body upright and the hips forward so that the weight is transferred onto the ski tails. As explained in chapter two, the stiffer ski tail, when weighted in such fashion, gives an exceptionally good forward slide, especially in bumpy terrain.

Tempo and Snow With differing snow conditions the racer must be prepared to adjust his tempo and technique to maximize his speed. In dry, fast snow, offering a good grip and slide, an explosive kick and a long glide with full extension are best. The glide phase should be as long as possible, but it should not last until the ski slows to the point where excessive energy will be required in the next kick to maintain the speed. The glide should be held only until a moderate amount of muscle effort in the next kick will be sufficient to maintain speed. This sort of know-how comes only with practice and experience and it is only after many kilometres of skiing that one is able to sense these subtle changes in speed while using the various strides.

In wet snow conditions, suction on the ski bottom rules out a long glide because the slide is poor and the ski slows down quickly. Thus the skier must shorten the

A neutral body position—straight hip and
good extension

glide phase but quicken the tempo in order to maintain the necessary full extension. Less energy is applied to each kick, but by virtue of the greater frequency of kicks, one expends nearly the same energy per unit distance as on dry snow.

Tempo should also be increased when one has the misfortune of choosing the wrong wax and is thus forced to race on a slippery pair of skis. In order to get maximum grip, a quick, complete weight shift and fast tempo must be employed. If the tempo falls, one must kick off a slower ski, which requires greater friction. If the wax is slippery, then this friction is not there and backslip results.

Racing on soft tracks is another special case where skiing tempo must be adjusted. Even though the snow may offer good grip and slide, it is inadvisable to try to put maximum power into the kick because balance during the resultant long glide is hard to maintain. The soft snow in the track offers a very unstable base on which to balance and generally the ski will wobble, roll, or break into the track surface forcing the skier to stumble or to waste energy in regaining his poise. The best procedure in soft-snow conditions is to increase tempo and shorten the glide so as to balance on each ski for as short a time as possible. Even though the glide phase is shortened, the technique should not develop into a running motion. The skis must still slide on the snow!

Tempo and Terrain The application of skiing technique to terrain has been discussed thoroughly in chapter three. The competitor should become very adept at changing his technique to fit the requirements of the terrain and still keep up a fast tempo. There are a few basic facts to keep in mind with respect to tempo and terrain. One must always be evaluating the track ahead in order to plan how to keep up

tempo. At the same time he should be trying to ski in such a manner as to always maintain maximum contact with the snow to allow a good grip for the kick; that is, in bumpy ground he should not kick off the crown of the bumps but rather when the ski is on the relatively flat upside.

On the flats, which are deceivingly easy, the racer must consciously try to increase tempo by full extension and powerful kick. Too often competitors ease up on the flat because they find them psychologically easier than uphills and and their minds wander from the race. The best defence is to try to consciously and continuously increase the pace on the flat by keeping the mind tuned to this aspect. Only in this manner will the competitor be able to sustain a consistent and fast tempo.

On the uphills one must switch into the tight diagonal, enter the uphill with a reduced tempo increasing it towards the summit, and finally burst over the top and with a good strong double pole begin the descent on the other side. The arm work must be quick with one pole always contacting the snow to hold in case of backslip. The hips must be forward and knees bent to allow for a quick, buoyant sprint to the summit. Skis should slide straight up the slope and only under extreme conditions of poor wax or poor track should one employ the herringbone or lift the skis from the snow and run. Some race tracks are notorious for the need of herringbone, and if one knows in advance, he should practise the herringbone and try to become quick at it.

The toughest and most important part of the uphill is the last stretch to the summit and over the top. It is here that many races are won or lost. Everyone is tired at this point and it is the person mentally capable of commanding his tired muscles to push over the summit who will come out ahead. Many people temporarily give up mentally,

The double pole must be quick and
aggressive

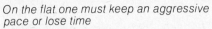
On the flat one must keep an aggressive pace or lose time

and then physically, under the stress and drop their tempo. Thus it is advantageous to practise driving over the top of the hills in training. Don't relax because the summit is in sight but push right over it and relax on the downhill side.

On the downhills one must be aggressive and confident. Much time can be gained over more timid competitors here. Downhills are also relatively free in terms of energy expenditure so it is wise to take advantage of them.

Select a good deep crouch and a good aerodynamic shape which doesn't catch much air. Even at the relatively slow downhill speeds in cross-country racing, air resistance is a factor in reducing speed. Keep the body weight as much on the tails of the skis as possible without jeopardizing the balance. In bumpy downhills of little pitch, press the weight into the hollows and unweight slightly on the crowns of the bumps. This pumping action will increase forward speed considerably on larger bumps at higher speed. The knees should flex and press the body weight down on the crown of the bump to prevent the natural tendency to become air-borne. One must decide whether to weight or unweight on the bumps by assessing his speed and calling on his experience.

Racing and Equipment

Racing equipment is essentially the same as the regular cross-country skiing equipment except that it differs in qualities such as lightness, strength, and durability. In addition, there are also some technical adaptations to serve the needs of the competitor.

Skis Skis made for competition are light but fragile and are designed for use

principally on a well-prepared track. Usually they have considerably more flex than the average ski in the tip and will have better quality wood on the bottoms.

Most top quality racing skis now have special synthetic epoxy-tar bottoms, commonly called black bottoms. Although the advantage of such bottoms over wood bottoms is questionable in cold, dry snow, they have proved to be superior in moist and wet snow. Being completely waterproof, the epoxy-tar will not suck up moisture to make the skis heavier or cause the wax to flake off when the wood beneath gets wet. Thus very few international racers are without black-bottomed skis.

Fiberglass skis have also come into the international racing scene and for wet conditions seem to be superior to even black-bottomed wooden skis. In fact it will not be long, according to ski manufacturers, before there will be two or three different skis of various flexes and types of soles for the different snow conditions such as powder, slush, and ice. Indeed, it is necessary for the serious competitor to keep up with technological innovations, but it is also necessary to evaluate them with regard to their contribution to increasing performance. Not all technological innovations are in fact advances.

Regardless of material or fabric, the ski must still perform in the same manner on the same snow as in the past, so it is important to review the qualities of a good ski outlined in chapter two. Of paramount importance to the racer is that he gets a ski that is the exact stiffness for his weight. Without proper strength the ski may slide poorly or slip. The wax will not wear evenly and parts of the ski will become bare of wax early in the race.

The competitor must also have confidence that his skis are the right size and flex and of the highest quality. He should select from only one brand of skis

A well-mastered herringbone can be a decided asset

and employ a few pairs both in training and racing until they become comfortable and familiar. Each brand of ski has a slightly different feel, balance, and flex and he must select the one for him and stay with it. Confidence is also generated by keeping equipment in good shape. If a competitor knows that his equipment is performing optimally, then he can put full concentration on the race and its demands.

Poles   Although skis are the most important part of the racer's equipment,

there are some considerations to be made about poles, boots, and clothing as well. As to the poles one should train and race with the same brand and employ two lengths, one longer pair for flat tracks and a shorter pair for hilly tracks. The height difference between the two pairs shouldn't be any more than 3 to 4 centimetres.

Boots   The racer should have two pairs of light boots for use in training and racing so that he has a pair of dry ones when the others get wet. A pair of rubber and wool boot pullovers are also a good investment to keep the boots dry in slushy tracks and to keep the feet warm in very cold weather.

Clothing   Clothing for racing should be light and windproof and the amount of clothing worn will vary with the weather and the individual. String vests are good in that they allow sweat to evaporate into the air space that they provide between body and ski suit. Plastic bags can be used to break the biting force of the wind on the knees and other vital areas. Surgical masks can be used in extremely cold weather to prevent frostbite on the lungs if one must train or race under such conditions. Finally a warm-up suit is a necessary piece of apparel for comfort during pre-race and post-race activities.

Race clothing should be geared to the temperature, the length of race, and the wind. One must wear more clothing in cold temperatures and for longer races where there is a higher risk of running low on water and sugar. Likewise on windy days when the wind chill is great it is advisable to wear extra clothing. Experience will dictate how much clothing one needs for various conditions, but generally it is better to be a little on the warm side when racing rather than to risk muscle cramps from the cold.

Preparation to Race

Travel   The competitor must plan his travel itinerary to arrive before the competition by at least a day in order to check over the condition of the track and become familiar with the snow. Be sure that reservations on public transport are arranged early so that no last minute problems prevent the arrival at the race site in good time. Travelling is one of the worst possible things that a well-trained athlete can do. Cramped sitting quarters, lack of sleep, long airport waits, hurried meals, time changes and cigarette smoke all contribute to a general malaise and ill-feeling

commonly called jet-lag. It can be reduced somewhat by doing light work en route such as walking outdoors or performing loosening exercises.

Because the athlete has little in the way of natural insulation, it is wise for him to dress fully when waiting around outside for taxis or other transportation. The stress of travel and exposure to a new cross-section of viruses can quickly result in a cold or the flu. For this reason one should never travel immediately after a hard race unles it is absolutely necessary. If you must travel, then relax as much as possible, keep warm, and be sure to replenish fluids, vitamins, and food consumed during the race as soon as possible.

Acclimatization   On the day before the race the competitor should ski easily around the track always trying to visualize how it will feel at full speed. He should run each downhill at top speed as he would in the race and try them again if he feels uneasy about them. It is important for him to leave the track feeling confident that he can master its most difficult parts with ease.

Apart from becoming accustomed to the track and snow, the skier must also adapt to environmental conditions if they are different from his home or training area. This is particularly true when athletes go from low altitudes to high altitudes to compete where oxygen and overall air pressures are lower. Although it is easier to breath at high altitudes, the aerobic capacity is reduced and thus distance athletes are impaired considerably. Observations made at the Mexico City Summer Olympics (7400 feet above sea level) showed that the average immediate impairment in maximal oxygen uptake was about 16 per cent and after 19 days of acclimatization it still approached 11 per cent.

At high altitudes the heart rate increases

but the stroke volume decreases. The breathing rate increases and the anaerobic engine comes into play more quickly; the athlete becomes less able to withstand high blood lactate levels after a few weeks. Thus if an important race is to be held at high altitude (above 3500 to 4000 feet), then the skier must act on one of the following two possibilities.

If he has not the opportunity or time to train at high altitudes, then the best approach is to arrive the day before the race and take it easy until the race. He will still be at a slight disadvantage compared to the acclimatized skier, but at least his blood lactate levels will still be low and he will be able to incur a larger oxygen debt in the race than if he had been at the site for a longer period.

To really become acclimatized one must be prepared to spend at least three weeks at the site. Further time spent gives only very small improvement, hardly discernible from daily variations in aerobic power. After three weeks, the heart rate will have returned to normal, blood hemoglobin will have increased, respiration rate and volume will have increased to fit the conditions, and the aerobic system will have adjusted to the lower oxygen concentrations.

During high altitude training one should practise a slower tempo and duration of activity. Recovery from intensive efforts takes longer than at sea level and the athlete will also want to ingest more food and water. Physiological and psychological response to high altitude varies from one individual to another. For some it is a heavy, unusual feeling of fatigue and for others it is a light, flighty, weak feeling of buoyancy.

There is no evidence that training at high altitudes, higher than the actual competition, is beneficial. In fact, it may have deleterious effects in that a return to lower altitude requires more energy to maintain the high respiratory rate acquired in the lower pressures of the higher altitude.

The Night Before Supper on the night before the race should be a high energy meal rich in carbohydrates. In fact if the race is an important long one you should have prepared by overstoring carbohydrates as outlined in chapter seven. Before turning in you should be sure that your equipment is in racing shape and laid out in order so that nothing will be left behind. A good idea if possible is to phone the local weather office to find out how the weather is holding. A falling barometer usually heralds the arrival of warmer and possibly stormy weather, whereas a rising barometer signifies clear, cold weather. With this information you can make some preliminary decisions on waxing.

Sleep may not come early and many such afflicted persons find that a light jog before bed will help to ease pre-race tensions. If you have a restless night, do not be too concerned because the sleep that you get the night before the race will not have much effect on your performance. It is the training and rest that you have accumulated over the weeks prior to this day that will count.

Race Day On race day rise early and give yourself ample time to eat and prepare. Breakfast should be light, non-greasy food and should be eaten at least two hours before the start. Pre-race eating is a personal thing. Some people can race with virtually anything in their stomach while others cannot eat at all. One classic example occurred before a 30-kilometre race when a certain competitor arrived late without having had breakfast. Feeling that he really should have something in his stomach for such a long race, he gulped down a hot dog and a coffee, the only food available. He then waxed and went out to thoroughly trounce everyone in the field.

Generally speaking, hot dogs are not recommended, but it is a good idea to have something solid for breakfast, such as porridge or other cereals. The food tends to raise the blood sugar levels, gets the system working, awake, and ready for action. If you have trouble eating in the morning, you should plan to begin with small amounts and eventually train your stomach to accept food, especially on race day. Large amounts of sugar should be avoided just prior to the race. By ingesting sweets in large quantities, one can actually decrease the concentration of blood sugar and in fact reduce the amount of fuel available.

One should plan to arrive at the race site at least an hour before start time. To prevent forgetting necessary equipment at the motel, establish a mental checklist to ask yourself each time you leave for a race. A simple "wax, skis, poles, and boots" will suffice for with all of these items you can carry on and race.

On arrival you should get your bib number as soon as possible and tie it on with knots, loose enough to allow easy breathing but tight enough to prevent shoulder straps from interfering with arm motion. Next get right down to waxing and trying out skis for slide and grip.

Before the start ski around for two to three kilometres to warm up. At least a ten to fifteen minute warm-up period is necessary to get muscle temperatures up to ensure a good metabolic rate and oxygen exchange. Warming up is particularly important in the shorter races and relays where a fast start is necessary and where the skier may go into oxygen debt if the aerobic engine has not been warmed up. At five minutes to go you should begin to take off your warm-up suit and at one to two minutes to your start you should be ready. Too often racers miss their start through poor organization of time prior to the race. After a year of preparation, it is ridiculous to blow it right at the start.

Waxing to Race

Waxing to race is really no more difficult than to wax for touring except that one must have a thorough knowledge of the different brands and their limitations. Waxing has been covered in great detail in chapter four and for the competitor it is necessary to be extremely familiar with the principles outlined there. Even so there are a few extra suggestions which can be made here which apply particularly to the racing situation.

Preparing the Ski   On the eve of the race one should clean all old wax from the ski soles and edges with a torch and steel wool. If there is a chance of crusty snow in the morning then it is wise to apply the base wax (binder) at this time so that it will set overnight to provide a faster surface the next day. On race day, if new snow has fallen, then it is no great chore to remove the base wax with torch and rag.

Weather and Snow   Keep an eye on the weather by checking the temperature over two or three hours on the morning of the race. Measure both snow and air temperatures and check to see if they are holding steady or fluctuating. If temperatures are rising, as they usually do in North America until noon or 2:00 p.m. then you will want to wait until the last minute and wax for conditions as close to the start time as possible. With fast rising temperatures it may be necessary to estimate conditions for an hour hence and wax for them, but keep in mind that snow temperatures lag behind air temperatures. Also you must build into your wax choice the fact that temperatures change with elevation; you should consider the possiblity of powder snow in higher sections of the track even though you may be starting in moist conditions.

Remember as well that snow changes with wear from skis so it may be necessary to use a softer wax if you are far back in the starting list. Spring is a tricky time for this type of change when fine moist snow blows into the track which has been cut into coarse, granular corn-snow. While testing your wax, you will find that hard waxes such as purple or yellow will work well but bear in mind that after the passage of numerous competitors the ice granules come through the fine snow and klister may be required.

Running Wax   Once you have ascertained the range of running wax for the conditions, you should decide on which brand within the range works best by trying them. Wax two pairs of skis or individual skis with various combinations and brands and then select a small downhill and check the relative slide of each wax job under equal conditions. Testing of wax by skiing one to two kilometres and matching slide in downhills is a very important process for the competitor where it is necessary to obtain optimum slide with good grip. Waxing several skis is hard work and many competitors would rather wax once and try to "patch up" problems by adding more wax; the result is a very slow ski.

Once you have achieved a slide and grip to your satisfaction, get the skis marked and then place them upright where the water from a roof doesn't drip on them or the sun doesn't shine directly onto the wax. The sun will heat the ski, and when it is again placed onto the snow, icing problems may develop. Never leave the skis on the snow and do not stand around on klistered skis before the start. Keep them moving so they will not ice up.

On problem days have your wax kit near the track with torch and waxes handy. Get your coach or a friend to be ready with the kit in case you must stop and change the wax or add some more. The rules of cross-country ski competition specify that the competitor can stop to change wax. He may be handed the wax, torch and equipment, but he must apply the wax himself. For races that cross lakes or streams known to flood in winter, you might as a caution carry a small knife or scraper in a pocket to remove possible ice from the ski soles.

Waxing Synthetic Ski Soles   Synthethic epoxy-tar skis soles are very slippery and must be waxed with care. They do not hold wax as well as wood and tend to allow more backslip with a given wax. To remedy these problems you will have to wax first with a tough cold wax such as Rode or Swix special cold green. Heat it and cork it well, then put on the running wax. The cold special provides a binder to hold softer running waxes. If conditions are granular, then base wax must be used just as for wooden-soled skis. Because the epoxy-tar surface is so slippery, you may well have to use a slightly warmer wax combination to get the desired grip, but this will vary depending on the brand of ski. For klister conditions there is no problem because the klister is tenacious enough to hold onto the sole without extra binding agents.

In-Race Strategies

There is a certain amount of strategy in achieving a good race result. A good race result does not just happen. It is the product of being able to put to use the training and expertise at one's disposal, bringing all together at the right moment in a well-integrated performance. Outlined below are some of the aspects to be considered in trying to perform to the limits of your capacity.

Pacing Not everyone has the conditioning of a world, elite-class skier, yet all cross-country skiers must race over the same distances as the elite. In this respect it becomes necessary to pace oneself during certain parts of the race in order to perform optimally over the whole distance. There is no point in barging out of the start at top speed only to run into oxygen debt a few kilometres out. In longer races, to ski above one's capacity for the first half of the race usually means a weak finish or possibly the depletion of blood sugar which forces the competitor to drop out. Thus in long, tough races it becomes important to know the optimum pace that allows you to finish strongly. With increasing conditioning year after year, your optimum pace will increase so that eventually you will be able to ski at nearly full tempo for the whole distance as the elite skiers do now.

In shorter races such as 5 to 10 kilometres there is little chance of depleting blood sugar stores and going flat; therefore, one should ski as fast as possible pushing through the agony of the first few kilometres. If you have done your training, you will be able to generate and withstand reasonably large oxygen debts over such short distances. Even though you get tired, you know that it is possible to push through to the finish without going flat.

Passing When overtaking slower skiers ahead of you on the track you will want to pass them without too much delay. The rules of the race dictate that both skiers are allowed one half of the track in a passing situation, but commonly the overtaken skier moves out of courtesy to the side of the track and allows his opponent the use of the full track. Certainly this does not mean that the overtaken skier should stop to let the other pass. Even though at the side of the track the skier being passed should keep pushing forward.

The official signal that a skier wishes to pass is the word "track", but when one is in a near breathless state it is often easier and helpful to the breathing to simply grunt or exhale the word "hup" or "huh". In any event one should not ski up to and clatter on the tails of the skier ahead in an attempt to annoy him out of the track. Most skiers respond to a verbal demand for the track and most often a polite but efficient request saves time for both skiers.

In passing an opponent the object is to then get ahead as quickly as possible. By sprinting or picking up the pace as soon as you are past you can open up a gap quickly, thus demoralizing your opponent and preventing him from hanging on and possibly passing you later in the race. In passing someone who is nearly equal to your ability, you must select a spot to pass that will be to your advantage.

Uphills make ideal spots to pass. Call on your reserves and pass quickly in the uphill pushing over the top with as much speed as possible. Your opponent will not likely follow because along with the psychological setback of being passed he will not likely be able to summon enough physical energy to regain the momentum lost while being passed. Similarly, it is wise to pass an overtaken opponent at the top of a downhill rather than follow immediately behind. More than likely he will be overcautious on the downhill forcing you to brake and tense up to prevent a much needed rest. Generally it

*The racer must pace himself to finish with
a strong kick even after a tough 30-km race*

is best to select the terrain in which you feel that you are the strongest to pass. If you are able to ski very fast then the flats may provide just as good an opportunity for passing as will the uphills.

Mental Work　During the race one must constantly concern himself with the track ahead. You must look ahead on the track, think about what is coming in the next twenty to thirty feet and adjust technique and tempo to suit. Never look back to see where your opponents are. Usually the only results of looking back are a break in rhythm and balance and an increase in anxiety.

On the other hand you should not direct your attention to the opponent in front so as to lose sight of the track either. It is best to concentrate on attacking the demands of the track before you, rather than to concentrate on catching the skier ahead. You must always concentrate on being loose and quick, all the while adjusting your technique to maintain the maximum tempo possible without becoming stiff. You must always be aware of what your arms and legs are doing in order to maintain a good technique especially when fatigue sets in. Attention to details such as these will soon close the gap to the skier ahead.

In addition, you should seek out the spots where you can rest without losing speed. By varying technique to use different muscles in different parts of the race, you can rest both mind and body. Often it is useful to promise yourself small rests after tough sections; for example, to push hardest up and over a hill, promise yourself a rest over the brow. Nine times out of ten having the uphill behind you will provide such a lift that you will forget the promised rest and continue pushing through anyway.

Many skiers ski the first part of a race in anticipation of what is to come in the second part. One should ski each part of the track for its own sake and not be thinking about how to get up tough uphills or how to navigate treacherous downhills which are several kilometres ahead. Concentrate on skiing the terrain at hand as well as possible and ski the terrain ahead when you come to it.

Relay Racing　Relay racing, especially at the start, is very tough because everyone starts as a group and the racer can see immediately how he is stacking up against the field. Nevertheless, the race is popular with competitor and spectator alike because the outcome is more unpredictable than for individual races. Upsets are common; lesser skiers can turn in sparkling performances and elite skiers make mistakes.

Before the start you should ski back and forth along your starting lane to pack it and make it faster. Often your success on the starting leg of the relay will depend on your position in line coming out of the stadium or start field. A position far back in the field means that you must pass many skiers before getting to the front, a situation which costs time and energy. On the other hand you may not want to be first out if you know that you cannot hold the pace so you will want to position yourself close behind the leaders. In any case you must get out of the start quickly and a fast track will definitely make for easier going.

The foremost consideration in relays is to keep a cool head and not to get agitated. Some skiers are good on certain parts of the track and poor on others so it is important not to get panicky if your adversaries gain a few yards on the flat when you know that you can gain it back on the uphills. If you are sure of yourself, the distance, and your opponents, then ski hard out of the start, gain a lead, and try to hold

No. 53 displays courtesy in giving the full track

Tight conditions demand clear, cool thinking

it. But if you are doubtful that you can lead, hang back just behind the leaders until an opportunity presents itself for passing and taking the lead.

Halfway is usually the best place to make a move because by then the over-intense starting pace will have taken its toll. The early leaders will show signs of fatigue, the lesser skiers will have fallen back, and the elite skiers will have settled into good solid skiing. It is wise not to wait too long to make a move for position, because even

the most tired skiers will always be able to draw on hidden reserves to fend off challengers when the finish line is in sight. Jockeying for position is best done in mid race where the mental stress for most competitors is greatest.

If you are being pursued and must hang on, then be cool; concentrate on proper technique, try not to make mistakes on corners and bumps, and above all don't look back. With your muscles in an acid state from fatigue, you must concentrate on efficient skiing and keep in mind that the skier behind is likely to be just as tired and has the added burden of trying to close the

Relay changes must be efficient

The racer maintains forward motion even while drinking

gap. The change-over of the relay, where the starting skier finishes his lap and tags the next skier, must be efficient so that no time is lost. As the racer enters the change area, the waiting skier should begin to ski forward in an adjacent track so that when the tag is made both skiers are going at top speed.

Drinking in the Race As mentioned earlier it is necessary to replace lost fluids in order to maintain performance levels. One should begin drinking sweetened liquids early in the race at about five kilo-metres and at each five kilometres there-after. In races of less than fifteen kilometres racers don't usually drink, but in longer races drinks are necessary. Do not make the mistake of refusing drinks to conserve time, because in the end your speed becomes less and less as dehydration sets in. At that point it is too late for replenishing liquids.

The technique of drinking is simple but effective for maintaining some forward speed. Ski up to the station and slow down enough to accept the cup of liquid with one hand, allowing the ski pole to hang freely by its strap from the wrist, while continuing to push with the other pole and arm in order to maintain forward speed. The whole procedure is similar to the two-step variation where one arm is held aloft and rested while the other does double duty. When emptied, the cup can be dropped and you can swing right into the diagonal or a double pole.

Positioning of food stations and recipes for drinks are discussed later in chapter ten.

After the Race Immediately after crossing the finish line it is a good idea to keep skiing easily for one to two kilometres to warm down. Easy exercise helps the muscles relax and clear out wastes collected during hard work. Then put on a sweat suit to keep warm until you are able to shower or bathe. At this point you are low on resistance to colds and the flu and as a result you should avoid getting chilled.

Most skiers rest after a tough race before eating. A short nap or lie down allows the body to recover to the point where it can divert blood to the stomach to assimilate food without much effect. Before undergoing further exercise or travel one should try to eat and drink enough to replace vitamins, sugar stores, and fluids used or lost during the race. To travel without doing so increases the risk of sickness.

CHAPTER 10

Race
Organization

during the actual competition. Such planning may be done by an individual working alone, but when the day arrives he must have the help of others. Even the smallest race requires at least five, and preferably ten, people to organize and carry out the necessary work. To produce the smoothest operation these people should work as a committee from the initial planning stages until the final results are mailed out.

Race Organizational Procedure

The organization and production of a race requires a certain basic procedure. The following approach to the organization and staging of a cross-country ski competition is not the only approach as many adaptations and short cuts can be learned through experience to save time, money, and personnel. Larger races may impose additional requirements due to the greater numbers of competitors or due to the increased importance of the race.

The decision to hold a race comes first and is usually made by a ski club or an interested group of people, such as a winter carnival committee. Larger races such as national championships or international races are often bid for at the annual meeting of the ski association, whether zonal, divisional, or national.

The first step in fielding a race is to establish a race committee (see table 10.1). This committee should be made up of knowledgeable people who have some experience in the sport. The committee should meet as often as necessary to be sure that everyone understands the whole procedure. The competition will run more smoothly if each person understands where he fits into the whole scheme. The committee will be able to operate exceptionally well after a few races; in fact,

Whether large and international or small and local cross-country ski competitions require the same basic organization. In order to field a successful event, the organizers must plan well in advance and try to anticipate the problems that can arise

some race committees have successfully staged major championships with only a few weeks notice.

Selection of a race date is important. The first consideration should be the local climate. The race must be held during a period that normally has good snow conditions and reasonable temperatures. Climate varies considerably throughout the skiing areas in North America and so does the reliability of snow and weather.

Once decided on, the race date and start time should be forwarded by the race secretary to the agency that publishes the racing calendar, usually the zone or divisional office. If the race has national or international appeal, it should be announced in the national race calendar; if it is as important as the National Championships, it may be announced in the F.I.S. Bulletin.

At these levels the race is said to be sanctioned by the national body (The Canadian Ski Association or C.S.A. in Canada) or the international body (The Fédération International du Ski or F.I.S.). This sanction simply means that the race has met the requirements of the sanctioning body in terms of organization and race trail specifications. If the race has never been held before, it may be necessary to provide race course maps, profiles, and proof of organizational capabilities.

Early in the planning stages the race committee must delegate one member to be in charge of the track (Chief of the Course) to see that it is in good shape and according to specification. This may require work in the autumn before the race to remove brush and obstructions. With the coming of the snow the Chief of the Course is responsible for packing, maintaining, and setting the track prior to the race. He will obviously require extra help and he may need a small budget for equipment.

A final announcement and entry forms must be distributed by the secretary about three weeks prior to the race. The forms must be sent in sufficient quantities to clubs and zones within the geographical limits from which one expects the racers to come. Some forms should also be sent directly to active competitors. Usually there is

Table 10.1 Race Committee and Officials

For Canadian Senior Cross Country Ski Championships 1971

Chief of race and chairman	John Pettersen
Chief of course	Oinstein Vannebo
Chief of time-keeping and calculations	Gordon Sahline and Assistant Dene Knight
Chief steward	Ray Smith
	Albert Wheele
Secretary of race	Diane Pettersen
Technical delegate	Irvin Servold Assistant Bjorger Pettersen
Competition jury	John Pettersen
	Oinstein Vannebo
	Irvin Servold
	Eastern or Northern Rep.
	U.S.A. Representative
Time-keepers	Harry Baycroft, Bob Gaasbeek
	Paul Paulson, Dene Knight
Recorders	Kay Paulson, Gillian Falck
	Marion St. Dennis
	Anne Mari Gaasbeek
Starter	Les Cashman
	Assistant Paul Paulson
Announcer	Doug Bradley
	Lorne Glassford
Telephone communication	Rolf Arndt
Scoreboard	Gordon Sahline
Doctor	Dr. Carson, Dr. Maxwell Ski Patrol
Chief of check controllers	John Martinsen
Finish referee	Fred Wheele and Assistant Arvid Ruste
Charge of banquet	Ann Dekker
Charge of concessions	Randi Pettersen

a reasonably reliable communication network amongst active competitors and word of the race often travels this informal route.

The trail crew must set the track the day before the competition, if conditions allow. The committee then must make the draw for starting positions, and the secretary should type the start list indicating the order and time of start for each competitor. This is posted in the morning prior to the race.

One to one and a half hours prior to the start, the secretary should be on hand to distribute the numbers and collect entry fees if they were not requested by mail. The course assistants and the Chief of the Course should be on hand to inspect the track and to mark skis. Both skis of each competitor must be clearly marked at the start and checked at the finish. Only one ski can be replaced during a race.

One half hour before the start, the course checkers should man their check points at confusing or strategic points along the track to direct traffic or to prevent short-cutting. Each checker should have a start list on which he ticks off each skier's bib number as he passes, thus ensuring that no one gets lost.

At the same time the forerunners should leave the start to "open" the track before the racers to ensure that everyone will have the advantage of a well-packed track. If snow has fallen during the night, the track should be repacked and reset an hour or so before the race starts to allow it to freeze.

At start time, timers, recorders, referees, and course assistants should be ready. The start can be a mass start where the clock begins at the same time for everyone or individual starts at 30-second or one-minute intervals where a competitor's start and finish time are subtracted to give his elapsed time.

As the racers finish, the timers announce times from their watches which are recorded by the recorders in raw form. The course assistants must check the ski markings and collect the racing numbers if they are not disposable. Raw times are reduced to elapsed times by the recorders and the final result sheet is made up. During races having several laps, unofficial times can be calculated between laps and transferred to a large bulletin board to inform spectators of how the race is progressing.

While the competitors are in the race and immediately afterwards, the refreshments committee should be prepared to provide warm drinks to the skiers.

After the final calculations, the chief of the race should scrutinize the results to check for possible errors. During a predetermined period after the race, possible protests may be received and the competition jury should be on hand to deal with them. Usually one to two hours after the finish of the race the official results, signed by the chief of the race, should be ready for publication, and the presentations should be made at that time.

The meet press officer or public relations committee should forward results to the news media or have arranged for a photographer or press man to be present for the race and at the closing ceremonies.

The final task is left to the secretary who must forward the results to the zone, divisional, and/or national offices.

These are the basic events involved in the running of a cross-country ski competition. Some of the more complex activities are further discussed in the following sections.

Dealing with Entries

Entry forms for the competition must provide enough information and be explicit enough so that there is no doubt as to the nature, the time, and the place of the competition. Often entry forms are included as part of the notice of the race.

Table 10.2 Notice of Race

The 13th Annual Viking Invitational Relay Races

Organizer:	The Viking Ski Club, Morin Heights, P.Q.
Location:	Viking Ski Trails near Morin Heights.
Date:	January 1 & 2, 1972

Events:

Ladies 3 x 5 km	Juniors 3 x 5 km
Senior Men 3 x 10 km	Veterans 3 x 10 km (over 35)

Start:

Saturday, January 1, 1972, at 2 p.m., Viking Club House

Ladies 3 x 5 km	Juniors 3 x 5 km

Sunday, January 2, 1972, at 10 a.m., Viking Club House

Senior Men 3 x 10 km	Veterans 3 x 10 km

Entry Fee: $6.00 per team for Ladies, Senior Men, and Veterans.
$3.00 per team for Juniors.

Medals & Trophies:

Ladies:	1st. — Viking Gold Medal and Cup
	2nd. — Viking Silver Medal
	3rd. — Viking Bronze Medal
Senior Men:	same as above
Juniors:	same as above
Veterans:	same as above
The Lufthansa Trophy	to be awarded to the best men's team
The Smith-Johannsen Shield	to the best junior team
The Viking Trophy	to the best ladies' team

Presentation of Awards: On Sunday at 2 p.m. in the Trinity Church Hall in Morin Heights in conjunction with a banquet.

Entry Dead-Line:

Ladies & Junior Relays:	December 31, 1971
Senior Men & Veterans:	January 1, 1972
No Post Entries are accepted.	

Send Entries to: Robert Weiler, P.O. Box 57, Morin Heights, P.Q.
Tel: 514-226-2413

Accommodation: *In Morin Heights:* Bellevue Hotel, Tel. 226-2209;
Swiss Inn, Tel. 226-2009; Le Chatelet, Tel. 226-3042.
There are also many motels along Route 11 not far from Morin Heights.

Note: The relay races are open for club teams, school teams, etc. Teams from the zone, divisional, or national level may compete, but will not be eligible for medals and/or trophies. Racing or competitor's cards have to be presented by the competitors.

The location of the race can be either described or shown in map form. The date, the time of start, the classes and events, the fees, prizes, and the sponsors must also be explicitly displayed. In addition, there must be a statement about late entries, or post entries, for invariably there will be some.

The secretary normally sends out the entries about three weeks prior to the race and receives them by a predetermined deadline either at his or her own address or at a post office box. This address and a telephone number should be included on the entry.

The entry form should register the name, age, club, and status or class of the skier and a signed statement relieving the sponsoring club of any liability in case of accidents, thefts, etc. If a program is to be printed, the race committee may request short biographical sketches of prerace favourites or national team members who are competing.

Sources of accommodation, with telephone numbers and addresses, may also be given to help out-of-town competitors. Table 10.2 illustrates a well-planned and factual entry form and notice of race.

Classes

Race classes are usually based on age groups. The purpose of the different classes is to try to group individuals of approximately the same physiological maturity. Grouping skiers in such manner is particularly important with younger skiers where a difference of two or three years in age can produce an overwhelming advantage in strength and ability. Within age groups it is also possible to group skiers according to ability to provide some incentive for up-and-coming racers who are not really in the same league as the elite. Table 10.3 shows the usual class divisions.

Table 10.3

Age	Classes	Distance
over 45	Senior veterans ("Old Boys")	all distances
over 35	Veterans	all distances
over 19	Senior (elite A,B,C)	all distances
17-19	Junior (elite A,B,C)	5-10-15 km
15-16	Younger Junior	5-10 km
13-14	Juvenile	3-5 km
11-12	Midget	1-2 km
under 11	Mini Midget	1 km

Making the Draw   The purpose of the draw is to randomly and fairly assign starting positions to the competitors. In a mass start race, there is no need to draw for starting positions unless space is limited and two tiers of competitors are necessary. In the individual start, however, certain starting positions are more advantageous than others and each competitor should have an equally fair chance at the best starting position.

Later starting numbers are preferred because the track gets faster after the passage of several skiers and because one can obtain the times of the earlier skiers and thus have a target to aim for. The better skiers usually like to start after about two thirds of the skiers are finished. However, under some conditions it is better to be early in the start list.

To allow coaches some freedom to decide where they would like their best and worst skiers to start, the race can be seeded. Seeding involves the division of the entries into groups. For example, in a race of 90 entries, there might be three groups of 30 skiers each. Each group has a separate draw for starting position within the group. The coach (or the competitor in the absence of a coach) decides in which group it might be best to start and then submits his name or names for that draw.

All of the names for each seed, class, or for the whole race if it is small are put into a hat and one by one the names are drawn and matched to starting positions beginning with the last and working to the first starting position in each group. By assigning names to the last position in each group first, all of the competitors are given an equal chance at the best starting positions in the seed. The start position number will normally be the racer's bib number which he will wear during the race.

Post entries, those that did not come in on time, are usually placed at the front of the whole race entry. Thus it is wise to leave several open numbers in front of the first seed to accommodate latecomers.

For relay races it is necessary to draw for lanes. The same procedure described above can be used. The team numbers can be placed in a hat and drawn for position starting with the best, the centre lane, and ending with the worst, the outside lane.

After the draw which, for large races, is usually held the evening before the race, the race secretary must type up, copy, and display the starting list indicating a competitor's start number, name, club, and starting time. A statement should also be made concerning when and where the racing bibs are to be picked up. Usually they are given out at a convenient spot near the waxing areas or the start an hour to an hour and a half before the start of the first competition.

Racing bibs are usually made of cotton with shoulder straps and ties on the sides. The numbers should be large and easily discernible. Often a race sponsor will donate them; there is space for his name and advertising beneath the number.

The recorder in action

Timing and Recording

Along with track preparation, timing is one of the more important and most difficult procedures in staging a ski race. Timing and recording require a well co-ordinated group of alert people at the finish-line. The timers and recorders should be isolated from the spectators, competitors, and those environmental influences that may distract them from the race during critical periods when the racers are arriving on the course. Times should not be given from the finish line, and competitors should not be allowed to ask for times immediately after their finish.

The timers are involved in both the start and the finish of the race. At least two clocks (and preferably three or four) are synchronized and then started at zero when the first racer leaves the starting gate. If the start is an individual one, then the remaining competitors leave one by one at

*Timers and recorders should be shielded
from distractions as shown in this
photograph*

15-, 30-, or 60-second intervals. If the entry is large, smaller time intervals can be used to get all of the competitors onto the track before the first one gets back to finish or to begin the next lap. On the other hand, jamming as many starts into as small a time as possible is not efficient, because this will tend to create a tight group of arrivals at the finish line making it difficult to obtain accurate individual finish times.

As each racer starts, the recorder should note and record his starting number and time on a standard time sheet such as the one illustrated in table 10.4. Times are usually recorded in minutes and seconds to make addition and subtraction easier; thus the watches used should measure minutes up to at least 60 or even 120 for the lengthy events of cross-country ski-racing. Thus, on table 10.4 racer 48 begins at 24 minutes after the start of the clock, racer 49 at 24 minutes and 30 seconds after, and so on.

As a competitor approaches the finish line (normally the same line as the start except in tour races), the timers and recorders are alerted by a course checker a few hundred feet up the track. The course checker shouts or relays by radio the bib number of the competitor approaching the finish line.

When the racer comes into view, the chief timer calls out the minute and proceeds to call off the seconds until the racer passes over the finish line. His watch is not stopped, but is kept running for the entire race. At the instant when the racer's feet reach the finish line, a finish referee or the recorder will note the time announced by the timer and it is recorded as an arrival lap time or finish time if the competitor has completed the race. When competitors arrive at the finish in a tightly packed group, one or two of the other watches may be stopped to get split-second times and then restarted on an even minute of the master watch. At least one watch and preferably

Table 10.4 Timing Sheet

Name of Race: Canadian Championship
Sponsoring Club: Cross-Patch Ski
Length: 15 km (3 laps)   *Class:* Open
No. of Competitors: 60

Name and Club	Start No.		Lap Times (Min.-Sec.) Arrival	Elapsed	Total Time		Place
T. Cross		3	74:10	17:00			
Red Bud S.C.	48	2	57:10	17:04	Finish	74:10	2
		1	40:06	16:06	Start	24:00	
		Start	24:00		Total	50:10	
J. Doe		3	76:10	17:50			
Cedarwing S.C.	49	2	58:20	17:20	Finish	76:10	3
		1	41:00	16:30	Start	24:30	
		Start	24:30		Total	51:40	
I. Faski		3	75:00	16:56			
Polar Ski Club	50	2	58:04	17:01	Finish	75.00	1
		1	41:03	16:03	Start	25:00	
		Start	25:00		Total	50:00	

two should run for the duration of the race. The referee or an extra recorder should keep track of the order of finishing when the racers come quickly to the finish in tightly packed groups.

When the competitor finishes each lap, his arrival time is entered into the appropriate column and row against the lap number completed. Arrival times are subtracted to give the elapsed lap time or the time taken to ski the lap. For example, in table 10.4 racer 48 arrived at the end of lap 1 at time 40:06 and at the end of lap 2 with time 57:10. The difference, 17:04, is the elapsed time for lap 2.

On finishing the race the competitor's finish time is recorded and his start time subtracted from it to give his total elapsed time (50:10 for racer 48). His time is compared to that of other competitors and this determines his standing. Obviously the lowest elapsed time wins the competition.

For extremely accurate timing the average of at least two watches stopped on the arrival of each competitor or electric timing should be employed. Accuracies of one tenth to one hundredth of a second can be obtained in this manner.

Race Results

From the timing sheets explained above, the race secretary should make up a result list arranging the competitors in order of their total elapsed times from the fastest to the slowest as in table 10.5. In addition to information about the competitor, i.e., his finish position, start number, name, division or club, lap and final times, some information on the temperature, general weather, and course conditions should be included. When interpreting such results, a coach or knowledgeable skier will be able to make use of such information in rationalizing performances and times.

Course information should include statements of total climb (MT), difference in elevation between the highest and lowest point (HD), and the maximum climb in one go (MM). Such information gives one an idea of the difficulty of the course and the type of demands put on the racer, thus giving some perspective to the times.

For spectator appeal unofficial times can be taken from the timing sheets as the racers complete their laps or races; these can be marked on a large bulletin board. Such boards have proved to be very popular at almost every ski meet. Their format can be identical to that for the timing sheet.

Before copying and publishing the results, the chief of the race should review the times and placings with the competition jury and if correct sign his name to them. The list is then published as the official results of the competition.

A typewriter and ditto copier should be available to publish results as soon as possible. Competitors like to know immediately how well they have done. In fact the result list is often more important to the competitor than are the prizes or trophies, probably because it represents the culmination of the long and lonely hours of training and hard work completed in the previous fall and summer.

Prizes and Awards   Prizes and awards will vary depending on budgets and sponsors. Prizes should be awarded to the first three in each class. It is always a good idea to announce the prizes and awards in the race announcement.

Annual races often have a large trophy on which winners' names are engraved each year and which is kept in a club house or showcase. In such cases the winning competitor is given a smaller replica or token trophy of the larger one.

Ski equipment or merchandise are good prizes in that they can be useful items and can also be provided for the race by a wide variety of sponsors. Such prizes should be matched to the class of skier competing. It would hardly do to award an elite racer a

Table 10.5   National Junior Nordic Championships

March 6-12, 1972
Middlebury College Snow Bowl

Boys 10K Cross Country—March 8

Competition Jury: Harry Brown, Technical Delegate; Steve Williams, Eastern;
Jim Burkholder, Alaska; Jim Ross, Chief of Competition;
Sandy Witherell, Chairman of Course.

Course Information: Length: 10 Km MT: 246.50 M HD: 61 M MM: 49 M

Pos.	Bib	Name	Division	5K Time	Total Time	Points
1	23	Bill Koch	Eastern	15:47.51	32:35.72	220.0
2	27	Tim Caldwell	Eastern	16:10.03	33:41.37	206.8
3	67	Ernie Lennie	Canada	16:36.10	34:01.99	202.8
4	31	Tom Siebels	Alaska	16:44.00	34:21.58	198.8
5	19	Pete Hamilton	Central	16:51.80	34:25.36	198.0
6	59	Dan Keenan	Rocky Mountain	17:04.92	34:29.28	197.2
7	26	Bill Strutz	Alaska	16:53.58	34:43.67	194.4
8	64	Mike Kuss	Rocky Mountain	17:13.88	34:43.81	194.4
9	16	Bob Tichenor	Alaska	16:57.63	34:55.18	192.2
10	61	Angus Cockney	Canada	16:59.91	35:04.82	190.2
11	57	Joe Lamb	Eastern	17:22.64	35:06.10	190.0
12	63	Jim Crawford	Eastern	17:15.57	35:11.28	188.8
13	10	Andy Hess	Alaska	17:01.58	35:18.22	187.4
14	52	Ernie Meissner	Pacific Northwest	17:10.83	35:23.91	186.4
15	66	Rex Cockney	Canada	16:59.38	35:32.10	184.8
16	48	Trygve Rler	Eastern	17:26.18	35:32.50	184.6
17	56	Steve Skaro	Rocky Mountain	17:51.37	35:34.83	184.2
18	17	Stan Dunklee	Eastern	17:08.43	35:41.11	183.0
19	60	Tom Springer	Alaska	17:38.48	35:49.22	181.2
20	65	Doug Hodel	Alaska	17:26.76	35:50.73	181.0
21	45	George Kitson	Alaska	17:50.49	35:57.13	179.8
22	36	Dale Carr	Alaska	17:41.49	36:03.92	178.4
23	55	Martin Hagen	Intermountain	17:55.03	36:06.97	177.8
24	68	Britt Lovelace	Rocky Mountain	17:33.16	36:17.67	175.6
25	70	Jim Galanes	Eastern	17:56.36	36:28.44	173.4
26	51	Craig Ward	Eastern	18:03.09	36:44.83	170.2
27	38	Mike Gleason	Rocky Mountain	17:53.77	36:46.25	169.8
28	40	John Downey	Northern	17:51.20	36:50.85	169.0
29	3	John Adamson	Alaska	18:03.92	36:51.87	168.8
30	20	Phil Peck	Pacific Northwest	18:17.35	37:09.47	165.2
31	12	Fitz Neal	Rocky Mountain	17:49.14	37:15.71	164.2
32	33	Rod Crawford	Rocky Mountain	18:36.06	37:25.86	162.0
33	46	Andy Moerlein	Alaska	18:30.97	37:26.68	161.8
34	58	Hugh Owen	Pacific Northwest	18:17.06	37:26.99	161.8
35	47	Jack Turner	Rocky Mountain	18:32.28	32:30.33	161.0
36	24	Mark Pasic	Rocky Mountain	18:07.55	37:34.10	160.4
37	69	Greg Fisher	Eastern	18:42.94	37:41.21	159.0
38	62	Rusty Scott	Intermountain	18:20.11	37:45.84	158.0
39	11	Dave Vanek	Central	18:20.39	37:49.33	157.2
40	35	Chris Weber	Canada	18:15.40	37:59.17	155.4
41	1	Pat Harmon	Alaska	18:34.96	38:02.84	154.6
42	5	Greg Crawford	Rocky Mountain	18:23.28	38:13.20	152.6

pair of new touring skis, whereas the same skis might be an excellent and appropriate award for a touring-class winner.

Prizes are a memento of the race and should be inscribed to give such pertinent data as the date, name of event, and placing. Such information is far more important than the size or showiness of the trophy. In fact, the result list is usually far more treasured because it tells the whole story of the competition. Nevertheless, the importance of awards cannot be played down entirely, especially for younger competitors who derive tremendous reinforcement from the recognition they receive as they ascend the podium to receive their award.

The Race Track

Next in importance to accurate timing and the publication of results is the preparation and setting of the ski track or trail. The track is the responsibility of the chief of the course and his trail committee. Their preparations must begin many months prior to the race.

The race track, whether it be a part of a trail system or a loop on its own, should be laid out, cleared, and levelled in the summer. All major obstructions such as trees, windfalls, humps, and rocks should be removed to produce a relatively smooth-surfaced track. Side hill sections should be cut in, so as to provide a platform for the track. The surface of the track should be level and smooth enough for use with minimal amounts of snow in the late fall and early winter. In addition the track should be prepared and designed for use without danger during the most adverse conditions, such as those following freezing rain or an extensive thaw. If the track is well prepared, it can also be used as a training track in summer and fall.

Ski Track Dimensions   Every track, especially if it is to be used for racing, should be measured for length and vertical variation. Measuring length is easily done with a tape, but vertical variation is a little more difficult to measure. Elevations can be taken with an altimeter at specific measured intervals along the track; they can be plotted in a long sectional form to produce a course profile (figure 10.1). If greater accuracy is required, a theodolite or level should be used to establish elevations along the track relative to a known benchmark.

If large scale maps are available for the area where the track is to be located, elevations can be obtained by noting the values of the topographic contours crossing the track which have been drawn onto the map. When air photographs are available in blown-up form, they can also be useful in locating the track.

Ski tracks can be of any length, but in some combination they should provide the desired standard race lengths outlined in table 10.6 for the various classes of skiers. Likewise, cutoffs and shorter loops should be available for younger skiers as described earlier.

Vertical dimensions are also given in table 10.6 as maximum allowable values for world and Olympic championships. Needless to say, not all race courses must meet these requirements. It is possible, although not always desirable, to hold races in parks, on lakes, or in flat fields with no vertical relief whatsoever.

The width of the track is also important. Enough brush and trees should be cleared to allow room for two skiers abreast thus ensuring sufficient width for overtaking and passing. A minimum width should be 10 feet on flat or even terrain and up to 15 feet on uphills where skiers might have to herringbone. In thick conifer bush a width of 12 to 18 feet is advisable in order to allow snow to fall onto the track. Heavy

TABLE 10.6 Course Specifications

Class	Length (km)	HD (max.)	MM (max.)	MT (max.)	Relative Difficulty
Senior Men	10 (relay)	200 M.	100 M.	300- 450 M.	2
	15	250	100	450- 600	1 (hardest)
	30	250	100	750-1000	3
	50	250	100	1000-1500	4 (easiest)
Senior Ladies	5	100	50	150- 200	1 (hardest)
	10	150	75	250- 300	2 (easiest)
Junior Ladies	5	100	50	150- 200	1 (hardest)
	10	150	75	250- 300	2 (easiest)
Junior Men	10	150	75	250- 400	1 (hardest)
	15	200	75	300- 450	2 (easiest)

Note: These are maximum values and are only a guide. Most domestic race courses fall well under these standards.

coniferous cover tends to intercept snowfall, especially early in the season.

Track Configuration   The cross-country racing track should consist of approximately one third each of uphill, flat, and downhill, laid out in such a fashion as to utilize the variety offered by the terrain. Sharp dips, steep pitches, and sharp turns should be avoided. The track must allow a skier to ski full out under all conditions with good rhythm; thus, steep climbs where the skier is forced to herringbone should be avoided as much as possible. Major turns should occur before and not immediately after downhill sections to prevent danger in adverse, icy conditions.

The degree of difficulty of the course must be geared to the level of ability of the competitors. The biggest climbs should be placed in mid race. Large climbs occurring right at the start do not allow the skier to warm up properly before entering into

heavy and possibly anaerobic work. Steep downhills near the end of the track should be avoided as well, because at this point tired legs could result in a fast, unplanned, dangerous trip into the brush.

The best track configuration is a loop design which begins and ends in the same place. Several possible variations can be used depending on the space and terrain available (see figure 10.1). One aspect of track design of prime importance is to plan the track so that there are a series of cutoff points for making shorter loops or to allow coaches to cut across and service their skiers at several locations during a long race.

The longest loop need be only 10 kilometres with cutoffs providing inner loops of 5 kilometres, 2 kilometres, and 1 kilometre, as shown in figure 10.1. In combination these loops can produce all of the official distances for all classes of skiers. For international races, the loops must be longer;

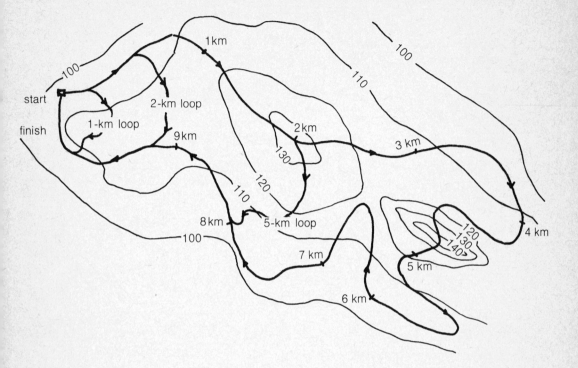

start

finish

1km

2-km loop

1-km loop

9km

2km

3 km

4 km

5-km loop

8km

7 km

5 km

6 km

100

100

110

110

120

130

120

100

110

120

130

140

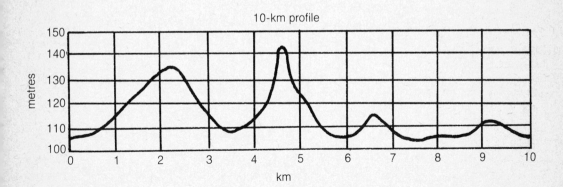

10-km profile

metres

150
140
130
120
110
100

0   1   2   3   4   5   6   7   8   9   10

km

Figure 10.1:   The Race Track

for example, there must be a full 15-kilometre loop, a full 30-kilometre loop, and a 25-kilometre loop which is covered twice for the 50-kilometre race. Needless to say, longer loops require more equipment and time to put into shape for competition. Shorter loops, such as 10 km or 5 km, are best for domestic racing as they are easily prepared.

Under adverse conditions a race can still be held by intensive preparation of a 2- to 5-kilometre loop and by increasing the number of rounds a skier must complete. Organizers should not make this the rule though. A 5-kilometre track should be the minimum loop around which longer 20 to 50 kilometre races are held in order to make an interesting competition for the skier.

Depending on the size of the entry and the type of race, the start and finish areas can be critical to the success of the race. For individual starts there should be at least two prepared tracks from the start line, converging at a distance of about 200 to 300 feet. With this arrangement two skiers can be started together in order to speed up the start of a large entry. If early starters begin coming through the start-finish line before the whole entry has been started, the extra track allows them to ski through without interfering with the timing or starting. Two tracks to the finish are also a must to provide each of two skiers, sprinting to the finish, their own track and equal advantage.

For mass starts and relay race starts it is necessary to have a larger area with many tracks or lanes converging at a distance of 300 to 1000 feet from the start. It is important here to be sure that all lanes are of equal length. Thus the starting line will no longer be straight, but will form a semicircle having a series of radii (the lanes) converging at a point some distance down the track.

Ideally there should be as many lanes as teams, but if there is not enough room then teams must be seeded into tiers. At least 10 lanes (preferably 15) should be set roughly 5 feet apart to accommodate entries of 10 to 30 teams. The starting skiers would then be arranged in rows 10 to 15 across and 2 to 3 deep with the best teams seeded in the first row and the poorer teams behind. For fairest starts each division, zone, or club should be allowed to have the starting skier of their best team in the first row. Thus the minimum number of lanes should be one for each division, zone, or club, depending on the level of the competition.

Where to Build the Track　Tracks are best built on controlled property where snowmachines and walkers can be kept out. Much work goes into the preparation of a ski track and all of this effort can be wasted by one wayward snowmachine. Firm and obvious signs may well have to be used to protect the track, even on private property.

In order to provide a maximum length of season, the track should be built in areas having a northerly exposure and be some distance from large lakes. The arrival and persistence of snow can vary considerably over a few miles in many parts of North America due to small variations in exposure, elevation, and vegetation. Thus it is wise to take into account the effects of these factors through an observation program over a few years before expending too much energy or money on a track.

Large open areas should be avoided because wind makes for some difficulty in keeping a track open in such areas. Treed terrain offers a wind break and prevents drifting. On the other hand, too much tree cover prevents snow from falling on the track. Thus the track must be planned to maximize both the benefits of climate and terrain.

Marking the Track   The track should be marked both permanently and intermittently for each race. Permanent markers can take the form of painted boards or squares of tin which indicate the main track by colour, letter, or number. Such markings can then be indexed on a main map or plan at the club house or start area. If there are several trails in the ski area, these can also be given a mark indicating their degree of difficulty for touring skiers. For example, an "A" trail is for racing, "B" for advanced touring skiers, and "C" for novice skiers.

Several days prior to each race and before the arrival of the competitors, additional markers should be installed. These markers should indicate the length and direction of the race. They usually take the form of arrows, ribbons, and kilometre signs. Kilometre signs should be placed at each completed 5 kilometres on longer 15-kilometre tracks with the last 5 kilometres marked at 1-kilometre intervals. If only a 5-kilometre loop is to be used, then each completed kilometre should be marked. Thus the signs would read "4 km", "3 km", "2 km", and "1 km" in the direction of the race over 5 kilometres.

The race markers should be colour coded for each class, especially when younger classes must cut off the longer loop. Each cutoff must be clearly marked both on the map and the ground. The skier may have his head down and be concentrating on the track, so the markings must be very obvious. Additionally, it is wise to place a course checker at points of interchange with a start list to help avoid confusion. Suggested colours, those used in world ski championship events, are given below.

Preparing the Track

Summer   Summer preparation includes the filling of holes, ditching, bridging, levelling, and clearing of various parts of the track. Equipment can include manual tools such as shovels, picks, and axes, and heavy machinery such as bulldozers for such larger work as cutting into side hills. The end result should be an unobstructed, levelled trail, smooth enough to run on comfortably without chance of turning or twisting ankles.

Winter   In winter, the trail should be packed from the first snowfall and with each subsequent one in order to build a firm, hard-packed base of snow on the track. This packing procedure is the only way to ensure that under warm conditions the bottom will not "fall out" of the track and that racers will not sink into it, thereby rendering it useless.

Tracks can be packed in different ways. Probably the quickest and easiest is to employ a wide-track snowmachine running around the track several times. Packing can also be done with skis and/or snowshoes. When a track must be skied in, it is best to set three skiers abreast to break down the fresh snow in a wide swath, thus ensuring a pole track as well. If enough skiers are on hand, several can come behind in the centre to "set" the track.

By far the best way of setting the track is to use a track setter made from plywood and hardwood blocks with metal cutters on them. Essentially it is just a plywood-bottomed box with an upturned snout. The blocks are bolted through the bottom and faced with metal. When weighted with

Race	5 km	10 km	15 km	15 km N.C.	30 km	50 km	Relay
MEN'S	—	—	Red	Green	Yellow	Orange	Green/Yellow
LADIES'	Blue	Violet	—	—	—	—	Red/Blue

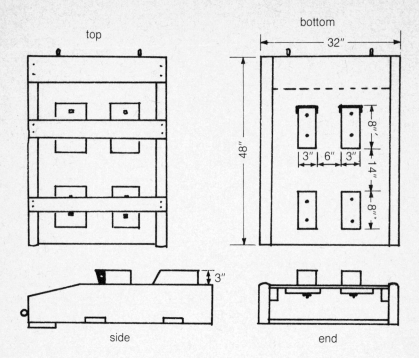

Figure 10.2:   The Track Setter (not to scale)

cement blocks or sand bags and pulled by snowmachine, such a device will cut into the snow to produce two sunken ruts or tracks in which one can ski easily.

The dimensions of the track setter are variable but can be of the order given in the accompanying diagram. The critical track dimension is the width of the dividing wall or centre between the two ruts and their depth. It should be roughly 5 to 6 inches wide, and the ruts should be about 2 to 3 inches deep. Thus the blocks on the track setter must be positioned to produce these dimensions.

The track should be set the evening before the race in order to let it freeze in. If the weather makes it necessary, it may be set just a few hours prior to the race.

On sharp corners and steep downhills, where a skate turn or snowplough may be

required, the track setter should be lifted and such places skied in. For best results a group of two or three skiers should follow the track setter to ski in the track. If this procedure is not followed, the first competitors may be disadvantaged because the bindings tend to catch in the tracks if only the track setter has passed over the course.

After intensive use, ski trails may develop a rather bumpy surface. Such bumps make for difficult skiing and should be smoothed by pulling a drag over the track. Concrete blocks, heavy chains, and other weighty items can serve to break up an icy track so that it can be reset. Two 2'' x 6'' boards with cross members nailed to them make a very good drag to level bumps and break up ice and crust.

Bottom of the track setter

Detail of cutting blocks faced with metal

Cutting a track

A good feeding station—the skiers are slowly sliding past

Food Stations

As mentioned in chapter six, skiers competing over long distances need to replace energy and liquid used while racing. Thus for races longer than 15 km it is essential to establish food stations at 5-kilometre intervals. The best location is in a section of the track where the skier can slide along slowly and easily without the use of poles. A slight downhill provides a spot where the skier can accept a cup and drink its contents without interrupting his forward progression.

The approach to a feeding station must not be too strenuous or too fast. A warm, sweet drink after a long gruelling uphill may make some skiers nauseous. Similarly, a long gruelling uphill immediately afterwards is not good either since the drink will divert some blood to the stomach and may produce a tired feeling in the arms and legs.

Equipment at the food station should include something to keep drinks warm and disposable cups. If the station is not too accessible and one must ski to it, then a packsack of thermos bottles is the best way to carry warm drinks. If the station is accessible by machine or car, a gas-fired camping stove can be used to keep the drinks warm. Drinks should be about 70° to 75°F. so that they can be consumed quickly.

The procedure at the food station is quite simple. At the appearance of each competitor some way up the track, the drink should be poured into a cup to about one third full. When the competitor arrives, the food station attendant should run along with the skier to give the cup over at the same speed so as to prevent spillage. A minimum of two persons should attend food stations to accommodate groups of racers who may arrive closely packed together: a drink missed early in a long race may cost the competitor many minutes later on.

Many recipes exist for the warm drink taken during a race. Usually it contains a certain amount of sugar and is based on some type of fruit juice. The sugar may be table sugar, dextrose, glucose, or honey.

An acceptable recipe uses such fruit as grapes, lignonberries, cranberries, or blend-erized blueberries mixed with an equal amount of water. A small shot of lemon juice, a touch of salt, and 5% to 10% sugar or glucose are added. The tartness of the fruit and lemon juices tends to nullify the overly sweet taste of the excess sugar and makes the drink more palatable.

Other Facilities

Essential facilities that should be provided near the starting area are waxing space, changing rooms, and toilets. Showers are convenient but are not a necessity so long as competitors are provided with space to change from their damp racing clothes.

When the competition involves two days and an overnight stay, the organizers may have to provide billets or suggest motel accommodation on the race notice. Buses should be provided to the race site if it is a considerable distance from accommodation; the bus schedule should be posted for all to see.

With a large entry it is often economically feasible to have a commissary established to feed both racers and spectators after the race. It may be possible to make money on the food to help defray the costs of the race or other club activities.

Index

Equipment
  basic, 12
  cost of, 12
  touring, 101-2
Exercises
  breathing, 153
  stretching, 152-54

Fiberglass skis, 170
Food
  before race, 173
  during race, 136-37
Food stations, 182, 202-3
Four-step diagonal, 55-57

Gloves, 45
Ground wax, 82-84

Heart rate, 133, 139, 145, 146, 161, 172
Heel plates, 32
Herringbone, 62-64, 147, 167, 195
Hickory sole, 14
Hollmenkollen, 124

Interval sprints, 146
Interval training, 144, 146-47, 157

Jogging, 145

Kick turn, 77
Klister wax, 85, 89, 91, 94, 98, 175
  applying, 92-93

Lahti Ski Games, 124
Leg strength training, 149-50
Lignostone edge, 13, 14

Marathon races, 117
Markers, track, 199
Mental conditioning, 158-60
Mental stress, 120-21, 158
Motivation, 160, 161
Mountain skis, 16
Muscle function, 134
Muscle training, 148
Muskoka Loppet, 107-9

One-piece bindings, 27
One-step double pole, 58
Overtraining, 158
Oxygen debt training, 144, 148, 149
Oxygen uptake capacity, 131-32

Paraffin wax, 90
Pine tar, 82, 84
Plastic skis, 95, 170
Poles, 37-41, 57, 58, 64, 71, 73, 77,
  150, 163, 171
  adjustments to, 39-41
  baskets, 38
  construction of, 36
  grip, 51-52, 94
  length of, 17, 39
Post entries, 190
Pre-season training, 158
Prizes, 193, 195
Programs, training, 154, 157, 159-60
Psychological factors, 158-60
Pulse rate, 133, 161

Race
  class divisions, 189
  clothing, 172
  distances, 118
  draw, 189
  drink during, 182, 202
  entries, 187
  facilities, 203
  finish areas, 198
  food before, 173
  food during, 136-37
  location, 189
  map, 197
  notice of, 186, 188
  procedure, 158-60, 185
  recording, 190-93
  results, 187, 193-94
  seeding, 189
  start areas, 198
  times, 118-20, 187
Race committee, 185-86
Race diary, 189
Race track, 120, 187, 195-96. See also Track